ELECTRIC RAILWAYS

OF LIVERPOOL
AND MANCHESTER

ELECTRIC RAILWAYS

OF LIVERPOOL AND MANCHESTER

GRAEME GLEAVES

AMBERLEY

Dedicated to the memory of Geoff Tucker and Dave Rimmer,
two departed friends whose enthusiasm for railways inspired my own.

First published 2015

Amberley Publishing
The Hill, Stroud
Gloucestershire, GL5 4EP

www.amberley-books.com

British Library Cataloguing in Publication Data.
A catalogue record for this book is available from the British Library.

ISBN 978-1-4456-3989-5 (print)
ISBN 978-1-4456-3994-9 (ebook)

Typeset in 10pt on 12pt Sabon.
Typesetting and Origination by Amberley Publishing.
Printed in the UK.

Contents

Introduction

There are few cities that have their names carved so deeply into the history of Britain's railways as Liverpool and Manchester, for it was between these two points, in 1830, against the backdrop of the Industrial Revolution, that the main-line railway story truly began, with the opening of the Liverpool & Manchester Railway. It had been built for the conveyance of both goods and passengers, such was the demand for traffic between these two great and fast-expanding cities. From that point on no one could doubt that the steam-driven railways would play an enormous part in the development of both our nation and its economy. And so it came to be, with hardly a village that was not within reach of the railways less than fifty years later.

Popular history will tell the tale of how the steam locomotive came to dominate Victorian Britain; how the railway mania created lines that radiated from cities across the country and fed the towns, suburbs and rural districts, many competing with each other. The same history will also tell of the decline of the railways in the twentieth century, of how the rise of the car and roadways exposed the limitations of rail, just as rail had cut short the rise of the canals before them, and how the glorious age of steam came to an undignified end in the 1960s amid a frenzy of unprofitable lines being closed and erased from the map and the steam engines going to their doom in scrapyards across the country. This left a reduced network of railways that have never been the same again, their golden age having passed. While some of this may be true it is a very one-sided view of history. Beneath that version there is another story, one of technical innovation and triumph, of the railways evolving to meet the needs of the future, to carry more passengers, over both long and short distance, and to carry them at both a speed and frequency that our Victorian ancestors could never have imagined. While the steam railway did indeed die out in the 1960s the electric railway was already a success story and one that would not only endure but would dominate rail travel to the present day and beyond.

Both cities owe so much to the Industrial Revolution and the resultant change that swept across Britain following it; Manchester became the centre of industry and Liverpool was transformed from a fishing port to one of the largest shipping hubs in the world. Neither city was slow to adapt to these changing circumstances and the region acted as a magnet for entrepreneurs, industrialists and inventors, not just from Britain but from much further afield. They were, like so many other Victorians, all eager to make yet more money, expand their empires or simply promote their products and developments. Britain was riding the crest of a wave of social and industrial change, and these were the personalities that drove it. While their individual motivations may have been in the most part driven by personal gain we can neither ignore nor discount that their contributions to the creation of our modern world have been far-reaching. This set of circumstances was very much in evidence in the story of the electrification of Britain's railways, for which we need look no further than the north-west of England, for it was here that another history would be made. It happened here first before anywhere else in the country. This book aims to tell the reader both how and why this happened: how two cities were to become the blueprint for so much of what is everyday across the rest of Britain. This is not a story of overnight change but one of trial and success as well as continual innovation, with the odd setback along the way. This volume is not intended to give an in-depth analysis of the technical details of any trains, power stations or current distribution equipment as there are more specialist works available for those whose interest lies in understanding these better. What I hope this book will provide you with is the background story that has for so long been overlooked and deserves better popular recognition.

Graeme Gleaves, Slough, England
Twitter: @mrlangelo

1

A Northern Soul

By the eve of the Industrial Revolution 30 per cent of the population lived in cities. While the nation's economy of that age was largely dependent on agriculture, industry was very evident. Coal mining had grown remarkably over the period from the mid-seventeenth to late eighteenth century and other minerals, such as iron ore, which occurred abundantly in the rocks below the nation, were also beginning to be exploited. The wealth of Britain lay not only in what she was able to produce within her borders but also in the control of trade outside of them. Britain had a long tradition of opening up trade routes, and had invested heavily in shipping. Subsequently, following a series of wars with France, the country had obtained numerous colonies, which had led to the creation of the transatlantic trade routes to the Americas and Caribbean. Britain was the major player in global trade and was getting richer off of the back of it. As the eighteenth century entered its final years, Britain was about to embark on one of the most significant periods of her history. Fuelled by inventors and those who saw a way to use their new creations, the Industrial Revolution came upon our isles and the way of life for everyone inhabiting the country changed forever.

The invention of the steam engine mechanised Britain's already prosperous mining industries and made them unimaginably efficient; their outputs rose to such a level that the country was producing as much coal as the rest of the world put together. The same could be said of iron ore, which gave Britain a head start in creating the metal that would build the specialist machines and structures of the new age. In the field of cloths and textiles there came a succession of inventions: the spinning jenny, the flying shuttle and the spinning frame. All of these brought mechanisation on an industrial scale to a manufacturing process that had previously been labour-intensive and conducted in small premises. But instead of replacing people with machines the new technology created greater employment, with more people operating the machinery to feed the needs for cotton, linen and textiles of not only Britain but Europe and the colonies. The cottage industry was no longer the way to manufacture these products; new larger premises with large workforces became the way forward – the age of the factory had arrived. With output raised substantially, so came the need not only to transport the goods from place of manufacture to the point of export but also to bring in the raw materials that the new industrialised Britain needed, such as the cotton that came from North America to be spun in Manchester. This job was first met by the canals, then in the early nineteenth century came the railways. At first these were considered a means for transporting goods in large quantities, such as coal, iron ore, slate and other building materials, but it was soon realised that they offered a way of transporting people too. With the rise in employment around industrialised areas came a resultant rise in population. Manchester, previously considered a market town, had a population of 30,000 in 1770, as the Industrial Revolution was beginning to take place in the area, which was becoming a hub of the cotton industry, with numerous mills and the factories opening. The district and its climate were considered ideal for the production of yarn. The population had, as a result, risen to nearly 200,000 by the time of the opening of the Liverpool & Manchester Railway in 1830. This brought about a huge demand for accommodation for workers, something the district struggled to cope with. Understandably the spike in population as workers flocked to live around their places of work resulted in conditions becoming cramped, and led to increased problems with sanitation, disease, pollution, and poor standards of living. This was in direct opposition to the greater prosperity that the Industrial Revolution offered the factory owners – a fact pointed out to Friedrich Engels, co-author (with Karl Marx) of *The Communist Manifesto*, when he visited the city as part of his research. The railways offered a solution to this: the railway was a means of transporting large numbers of people between the industrial areas and the residential ones, so suburbs on the outskirts of cities could be created. This in turn saw greater expansion of the cities, with districts that were previously separated from the city being swallowed up as more new housing was built. At first this 'suburban' dwelling was only for the wealthier members of society keen to escape the squalor of the city – they were the only ones able to afford to. With the increase in wealth for a percentage of the population came the need for better financial services, and many cities developed financial quarters, where investments, savings and insurance were managed. The template for city life for the next 100 years was quickly being drawn. As far as Manchester was concerned it could boast a population of over a quarter of a million by 1835, and its expansion showed no sign of slowing down.

While Manchester was fast becoming the centre of British engineering, Liverpool was also expanding way beyond the fishing port it had been in the early eighteenth century. Its economic prosperity had been down to its location as a key port for the Atlantic trade routes. The docks there had grown during the early eighteenth century as they handled traffic in coal, iron ore and other raw materials, such as cotton, timber, spices and, in the bleaker periods of British history, slaves from the colonies. While the latter trade stopped, the advent of the Industrial Revolution only placed greater strain upon the docks and resulted in further expansion. Like Manchester, Liverpool became prosperous, and a thriving financial district developed, along with a huge network of warehouses, customs houses and stores for the handling of

Route map of Manchester's rail network, showing the numerous companies involved in feeding into the city's two termini. (Creative Commons)

the thousands of tons of merchandise that passed into and out of the docks. This generated large-scale employment and resulted in the overcrowding of the city. The wealthier merchants used the railways as a means to escape those conditions, and headed north away from the city to the districts between there and Southport. Across the River Mersey lay the Wirral Peninsula, with the market town of Birkenhead. Industry had gained a strong foothold here; it was to a lesser degree but was significant none the less. Birkenhead could boast its own docks and commercial district, while housing was being constructed at the north end of the Wirral for those in a position to escape town life and the cramped conditions that blighted it. Most of the new housing that offered an escape from city life was driven by the construction of new railway lines radiating out from the city to the outlying towns and villages. With the railway's arrival came the chance to realistically live away from the city and travel to and from there each day to carry out your business; the new breed of professional, known as the commuter, was born.

By the mid-nineteenth century the pace of change had slowed little, but many social reforms had forced living conditions to be improved for workers in the industrialised cities like Liverpool and Manchester. More and more people were able to live further from the city centre and their places of employment. Britain was a fabulously wealthy country that now had a global empire with which she could trade goods. Much of that trade focussed on the port of Liverpool, which had continued to expand to become the second-largest port, after London, of the British Empire. It was originally run by a board of trustees, who held absolute authority over what did, and what did not, happen in the docks. This gave rise to corruption, with favourable terms and better access being available to those who knew the right people to talk to and how to convince them. However, beneath all this the docks were a huge success and made their owners a considerable sum of money; they kept expanding to meet the rising demand. This did not go unnoticed, and there were those outside the circle of influence over the running of the port who felt that the trustees of the docks were becoming far too powerful. In 1857 an Act of Parliament was passed that took the control of all future management of the docks away from the trustees and created the Mersey Docks & Harbour Board (MDHB). All of the success the docks enjoyed created wealth and employment for Liverpool itself; as the nineteenth century entered its final decade, the docks employed no fewer than 30,000 people, ran for a length of 7 miles along Liverpool's waterfront, and handled imports and exports whose totals were measured in millions of tons. It is with the success of the docks that our electric railway story begins.

A procession of horse-drawn drays and carriages line up alongside the electric tramway in Liverpool around the turn of the century. Visible above the streets is the structure of the then new Liverpool Overhead Railway. (Author's Collection)

2

The Long and Winding Road

Liverpool's Dock Road was one of the most important roadways in the British Empire in 1890. It was an amalgamation of individual roads that linked up to form a continuous passage along the length of the dock estate from north to south. Any person or cartload of merchandise needing to enter or leave the docks would have needed to pass along the Dock Road at some point, before heading off into either the city or routes further afield. Even following the advances of the Industrial Revolution, any commodities requiring onward road transport still relied on simple horse-drawn carts to be moved. Most workers moved on foot, and between all of this there was the Dock Road railway, laid into the street and served by branches into each individual dock, where wagons were loaded or unloaded with goods, and ferried away, often by horses, to transit points, where they could be handled by the main-line railways for onward traffic. Needless to say, the Dock Road was a busy place and an important one. A hold-up, due to congestion, that delayed the sailing of a ship could have repercussions in any point across the British Empire.

The idea to build an elevated railway above the Dock Road to relieve congestion was first proposed in 1852, prior to the formation of the MDHB, but the plans did not progress and lay dormant for a quarter of a century, when they were revisited by the MDHB, who knew that to do nothing was no longer an option if the future smooth operation of their concern was to continue. An elevated railway had by this time been built in New York, so the idea that it was viable was not without evidence. A Bill was put before Parliament for a single-track line, but the Board of Trade had reservations and insisted that any line built would need to be of double track. This stalled the project for a few years until a new Act was obtained in 1882 for a double-track line from the northern end of the dock estate at Alexandria Dock to the newly completed southern basin at Herculaneum. The line was to be worked by steam, and would feature tramcars similar to those horse-drawn vehicles that were starting to appear across Liverpool and Birkenhead. Despite the Bill being approved, the MDHB dragged their feet and no work was started. This was due in part to factions within the MDHB who were very opposed to the idea, and it was evident that despite the obvious need to do something to relieve the pressure on the Dock Road there would have to be some mediation to secure a way forward for the project. Salvation came in the form of an agreement that the railway would be built and operated by a company, independent of the MDHB, who would lease the ground it ran on and fund all the construction and operating costs from its own purse; and so the Liverpool Overhead Railway Company was created in July 1888.

The new company was headed up by a board of directors drawn from wealthy and successful merchants and entrepreneurs of the city. They set about raising the capital to have the railway built. Attention turned to the method of operation, and while the first sections of the steel structure were being set above the Dock Road, a significant event happened that would greatly influence the nature of the Liverpool Overhead Railway (LOR). In 1890 London witnessed the completion of the world's first underground railway, the City & South London. It was remarkable as being the first major railway in the world to be powered by electricity, with small four-wheeled locomotives hauling trains of three carriages. The principle engineer of the railway, James Henry Greathead, was also appointed as one of the consultant engineers of the LOR, and it was no coincidence that the LOR began to look seriously at this new form of propulsion for their trains. One factor that swayed them in favour of it was the reduction in fire risk from electric traction as opposed to steam; it has to be remembered that in the last decade of the nineteenth century, ships were still built of wood, with canvas sails. A second deciding factor was that of weight. The LOR was being built on a viaduct, made of steel girders, along almost its entire length; the deck was made of a succession of inverted U-shaped plates riveted together, and the electric trains being envisaged would have their weight distributed along their entire length, unlike a conventional steam-hauled train, where the majority of the weight is at the end where the locomotive is. Another factor in reducing stress on the elevated structure was the nature of the electric motor in operation – it exerts far less force upon the railhead than the piston operation of the steam locomotive does. The more the LOR looked at electricity over steam as their preferred form of traction, the more it made sense. Of course, there were risks; electric traction was still in its infancy, and despite the success of the City & South London Railway and a handful of tramways that had either converted to or been built with electric motive power in parts of Britain, Europe and America, the technology was still very much being developed, not just in terms of the equipment carried on the trains but also the need for electricity generation and a supply network to the railway. There was no national grid, and all the power needs of the line would have to be met by the LOR building its own generating station.

The LOR decided to take the electric option, and orders were placed for both trains and the equipment for the power station, the site of which was to be just over halfway along the line to the north, so that it had could easily be supplied with both coal and water for the boilers. The power station relied on steam in the

The LOR structure is clearly seen in this aerial view, following the line of the docks and separating it from the industrial landscape of the city. (Jim Peden)

A broadside view of one of the original LOR carriages. The driving compartment is on the left, with passenger classification marked on the remaining three doors. (Author's Collection)

first instance, with six Lancashire boilers being installed that drove the dynamos needed to produce the electric current at a pressure of 500 volts DC. From here the current was supplied to the railway by a central live rail mounted between the two running rails, and the negative return circuit was fed back to the power station by the running rails. This arrangement was identical to that employed on the City & South London Railway. To avoid current being leaked to the metal decking of the railway's structure, the conductor rail was carried off the ground by porcelain insulators, and the running rails were spiked to wooden sleepers, but unlike the traditional railway, where the sleepers were laid at 90° to the running lines, the ones on the LOR were laid longitudinally under the running rails.

Perhaps the greatest innovation of the new electric railway age that the LOR brought to the world was the make-up of the trains themselves. The trains were marshalled into two coach formations, and outwardly they followed very traditional construction lines, with teak-panelled bodies mounted on timber frames, which then sat on two four-wheeled bogies. The interior was plain, with wooden bench seats, not unlike a tramcar, and a small furnished section for first-class passengers. There was electric lighting, which was fed from the train's traction supply system. What made these trains so very different to anything seen elsewhere in the world was what was missing – there was no locomotive. Contained at the outer end of each car was a driving compartment, and beneath it on the leading axle was an electric motor of the gearless type, meaning the armature was wrapped around the axle; these motors were rated at 60 hp. The two motors on the train were directly coupled electrically, so the whole two-coach train was under the direct control of the driver. By advancing the controller, he could take both the motors through the various stages of resistance from series to parallel operation and accelerate the train to its maximum speed of 30 mph. Today, of course, it is the norm to board a train where the driving cab and traction equipment is all incorporated with the passenger carriage, but one has to imagine how it would have looked to our Victorian ancestors, experiencing these trains for the first time – rather like the first electrically propelled trams, which had run a few years earlier, with no horse before them. The trains themselves had been built by Brown Marshalls at Saltley in Birmingham, and then sent to the works of the Electric Construction Company to be fitted with their bogies and electrical equipment before onward transit to Liverpool. One advantage of this type of train was that it could enter a terminus station and be ready to depart on the return journey in no more time than it took the driver to walk from one end of the train to the other. On an intensively worked service, as the LOR was envisaged to be, the abolition of the need to run around locomotives, which would also need to be restocked with coal and water, was a saving in terms of time, manpower and infrastructure that could not be understated.

Electricity gave the LOR the chance to embrace another new technology that had been developed for the operation of urban railways: that of automatic

A very early view of an original LOR two-car set in operation. Note the position of the central conductor rail and how it was aligned for point work. (Author's Collection)

An early LOR train overtakes the horse-drawn traffic on the Dock Road below. The signal in front of the train is one of the early automatic ones. (Author's Collection)

signalling. The design had been patented in April 1891. In this new system, only the two terminus stations were worked by conventional mechanical signals. The intermediate sections were controlled by the passage of trains themselves. The signals were designed to be fail-safe, so the semaphore arms were held in the clear position by electromagnets, which meant that any failure of the current supply to them would immediately revert the arm back to the 'stop' position. Trains would trip levers on the track when departing stations, which would then switch the signals to 'danger' behind them, and that signal would not clear to 'proceed' again until the lever had been tripped for the signals in advance of it; thereby the system would not let two trains into the same section of line controlled by a single signal. The power for the signal lamps came from the power supply for the station lighting, with each station having its own independent supply point. The system worked perfectly for the LOR's needs and was really ahead of its time. In the following years automatic signalling controlled by the passage of trains would become the norm for nearly all Britain's railways, so the LOR can claim yet another influential first.

The construction of the railway continued apace during 1892 and into 1893, with the deck sections being constructed by a purpose-built crane that ran on the part-completed structure and laid new decking ahead of that which had already been finished. The only part of the line that was not elevated was a short incline needed to get the route to pass below a bridge that carried a coal line near Nelson Dock; here the line dived down under the railway bridge at 1 in 40 and then rose

The interior of the generator room of the LOR power station showing the belt-driven dynamos. (Author's Collection)

back up at 1 in 80 to resume its position of 16 feet above the Dock Road. In 1893 the final fitting out of stations and the completion of the carriage sheds at the northern end of the line at Seaforth Sands was achieved, along with the delivery of the rolling stock, which comprised thirty carriages, giving fifteen operational sets for the service. The grand opening took place before the Board of Trade sanctioned the opening of the line to the public. Lord Salisbury carried out the ceremonial switching on of the line in February 1893, with the formal inspection by the Board of Trade taking no less than four days to complete, due to the unusual nature of the line's construction and method of operation. All was completed and approval given for the public to be carried from 6 March 1893. Liverpool had joined the electric railway age, and in doing so had created a blueprint for the urban electric railway that was to be copied, albeit at ground level, many times over.

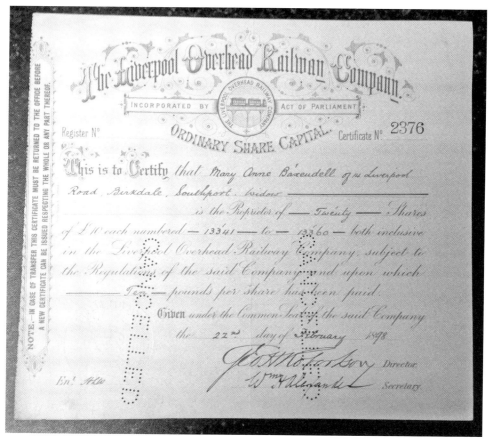

A share certificate issued in February 1898 to record the purchase of twenty shares in the LOR by Mary Anne Baxeudell, a widow from Southport. The subscribers to raising the capital to fund the construction and initial operation of the railway came from various walks of life.

3

Ferry Cross the Mersey

When the LOR opened for business, the residents and workers of the city embraced it as a welcome addition to their transport needs. However, there was one pair of eyes that viewed its clean, efficient electric operation very, very enviously.

Up until 1886, the ferry was the only direct route between Liverpool and Birkenhead on the other side of the River Mersey. Merchants and industrialists on both sides of the river had recognised the need for a fixed link that could run in all weathers between the two towns, and they formed a company in 1866 to build a tunnel under the river that would contain a railway operated by compressed air. The idea was that the carriage was pushed along the tunnel by air pressure, rather like a giant pea-shooter. The idea, unsurprisingly, proved utterly impractical, and no physical work on the construction began. Then in 1880 the scheme was revived, this time as a conventional railway tunnel carrying two tracks. The tunnel was to be wide enough for two tracks and lined with brick after excavation. The company, which by now had been renamed the Mersey Railway Company, had problems throughout the construction, with contractors going bust and alternatives having to be found to see the works through to completion. The contractor who eventually finished the construction did so only in exchange for a large share in the company, though this would-be entrepreneur did not live to see his profit, as he died only a few weeks after the railway opened. It appeared that the railway under the Mersey was cursed.

The Mersey Railway finally opened in February 1886, and ran from an underground station in James Street, Liverpool, under the river to Green Lane in Birkenhead. By 1892 the railway had reached its final length, extending through a further new tunnel on the Liverpool side to Liverpool Central station; on the Wirral side there was one extension north to Birkenhead Park, where the railway physically connected to the Wirral Railway, and another southerly extension to Rock Ferry, where the line connected with the Birkenhead Railway. These two later extensions enabled connection with the national network. It should have been the case that the much needed fixed link had a very bright and prosperous future; unfortunately that was not quite the case. Less than four years after the Mersey Railway had opened, its passenger numbers began to decline as patrons went back to the slower ferries as their preferred method of crossing the river. Why was this? The reason lay in the method of propulsion the Mersey Railway employed for its trains – steam.

When opened, the railway had gone to great lengths to keep the air in the tunnels as clear as it could. There were two vast pumping stations, one on either side of the river, that pumped clean air from outside down into the tunnel in an attempt to keep fresh air circulating in the enclosed environment. In addition, the steam locomotives that hauled the train were fitted with something called 'condensing apparatus', which was an arrangement of pipes that drew steam that would normally be 'chuffed' out of the exhaust chimney back into the locomotive; this steam was then cooled back into water and returned to the loco's water tanks. A major drawback of this is that it can make the locomotive less powerful, and as the line under the river had steep gradients at each end, this meant that the steam locomotives were working harder to overcome the disadvantage of the condensing apparatus. Condensing apparatus only dealt with steam vapour and had no effect on the smoke and soot created by burning coal on the locos. With a train through the tunnel in each direction every five minutes, the ventilation equipment was simply unable to cope with all the pollution the steam trains created, and down in the tunnels the atmosphere was described at the time as 'noxious'. The problem was not a new one, as any traveller on the underground section of the District or Metropolitan railways in London at the same time would testify. It was little wonder that passengers abandoned the new railway in favour of the ferries. By 1891 the railway was bankrupt, and in order to remain open needed to find a saviour to turn its fortunes around. The stage was set for the American cavalry to ride into town and save the day.

The Mersey Railway knew that they needed to electrify their services. Electric trains would produce none of the pollutants that choked the air in their tunnels and drove passengers back to the ferries, and they need only look to their neighbours at the Liverpool Overhead Railway to see the obvious advantage of electric traction. The only problem was that to both install the equipment and build the new trains that electrification needed, they would have to raise a lot of fresh capital, and the fortunes so far of the Mersey Railway meant it was not going to be seen as a sound investment by many with the requisite finance to invest. A saviour arrived in 1899 in the form of George Westinghouse, an American inventor and a shrewd businessman who had established a highly successful engineering empire in America and was now looking to set up a manufacturing base in Manchester to open up a sales market for both Britain and Europe. Westinghouse was approached by the Mersey Railway about the costs involved in re-equipping the line for electric traction, and he told them that he could not only provide the equipment to electrify their railway but also the know-how to make it profitable as a result. In return for carrying out the work he wanted a substantial share in the railway company. The Mersey Railway board of directors agreed to his terms; after all they had very little choice – their situation had declined to the point where their revenue no longer covered their operating costs – so an agreement was reached and the work commenced.

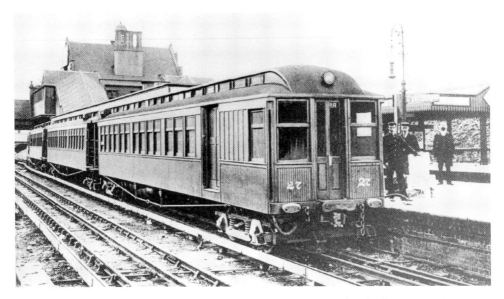

A three-quarter view of the Mersey Railway stock when new, clearly showing its American design. (Author's Collection)

Unlike the handful of electric railways that were operating in Britain at the dawn of the twentieth century, the Mersey Railway was already a going concern; those lines that had elected to use the new form of traction had done so from their creation, so a problem the Mersey Railway faced was carrying out the electrification work without interrupting the service they already offered. This meant the work had to be carried out overnight, which still offered a relatively small window, as the service ran from dawn until after midnight. Sundays offered more time, as the service did not begin until after midday. In addition to the installation of the conductor rails, there was also the task of giving the underground tunnels and stations a heavy clean, as the company wanted to use the advent of electrification to break away from the image of soot, smoke and dirt that had come to, not unfairly, blight its image. As with the Liverpool Overhead, the conversion of the railway to electric operation required the construction of a power station on the Wirral side of the river in Birkenhead. Domestic electrical supply on both sides of the river existed but was in its infancy, and no company could offer the supply of power the railway would need. The power station supplied electricity at 600 volts DC to a positive conductor rail laid alongside the running rails. The trains were equipped with collector shoes on their bogies that transferred the electricity to the trains' motors, and the negative return of current required to complete the circuit was fed back by additional shoes fitted to the underside of the bogies, which made contact with a negative conductor rail fitted between the running rails. The American money that was funding the project was very evident in the new fleet of trains that were ordered for the railway. They had the lines of a carriage straight out of a cowboy western movie, with

The saviour of the Mersey Railway, George
Westinghouse. (Library of Congress)

60-foot-long bodies mounted on bogies. The interiors were open saloon, with
square windows, clerestory roofs and automatic couplings. The bodies were built in
Shropshire by G. F. Milnes to a design supplied by the Baldwin Locomotive Works
of Philadelphia. One omission was that of heating, which was deemed unnecessary
as most passenger journeys were only a few minutes long. The braking system was
the Westinghouse air brake, with compressed air replenishing the system at each
terminus. The teak-panelled bodies were painted in a red livery with gold lettering
and numbers. The trains were lit by electricity fed from the traction supply. One
further technical advance they featured was the system of multiple unit control,
which had been invented by Frank Sprague in America and allowed one driver to
control all motor vehicles in a formation simultaneously. This was an advance on the
system pioneered on the LOR, which limited the formation to one two-car unit and
required an excess of high-current cables between the cars. The Sprague system used
a lower control voltage, and the electrical connection between the cars was made
by means of multiple pin plug jumpers for a much tidier look. The Mersey Railway
electrical multiple units (EMUs) set the benchmark for all of the first generation of
suburban units that would be introduced in Britain over the next two decades, in
terms of both appearance and operation. The fleet was divided up into twenty-four
motor coaches, each with a driving position, and thirty-three trailer cars. The non-
driving vehicle ends had a platform with a lattice gate that was opened and closed
at stations by a dedicated gateman to allow passengers to board and alight. Prior
to delivery to the railway, each car had to go to Westinghouse's industrial plant at
Trafford Park to be fitted with motors, traction and brake equipment. The training

of the steam crews to drive the new trains took place after the service had stopped, and must have been quite a culture shock for many of them, as in their previous jobs they were working in a dirty, noisy, hot environment and now they had the benefit of clean, quiet cabs, but perhaps the biggest change was that they now worked alone, as there was no need for a fireman to share the footplate with them.

All work, training and commissioning was completed during the spring of 1903. It was remarkable that the railway had continued to operate during the period of transition, and it simply was a case of the last train to run on 2 May being steam hauled and from start of service at 1 p.m. the next day a full electric service being commenced. All the steam locomotives and carriages were sent to storage at Bidston and were eventually sold on to new homes, not surprising as they were just under twenty years old and there was a healthy market for such items among the numerous light and industrial railways. The new service settled very quickly, and the Mersey railway entered a new period of rebirth, with patronage previously lost to ferries being reclaimed. There would be no road crossing of the river to compete with for a few decades, so it appeared the company had finally been lifted of their curse.

Interior of the Mersey Railway stock as built. This is third class. (Author's Collection)

A postcard of Rock Ferry station from 1905, showing a Liverpool-bound train at one of the Mersey platforms and a spare carriage, which will be reattached to a service for peak working, in the middle road. (Author's Collection)

4

New Direction

The two lines to adopt electric traction in Liverpool to date had both been smaller independent concerns, each running over their own short sections of line and not in direct competition with any other company for rail passengers. Liverpool was now a large, bustling and prosperous city, and of course this had made it a target for the construction of many lines during the nineteenth century. The larger railway companies had sponsored many of these or had bought up many smaller concerns to give them access to the rail market feeding the city. One such company was the Lancashire and Yorkshire Railway (L&Y), whose empire covered large swathes of both those counties. It was the third-largest railway company operating in the north of England, and had been formed by the amalgamation of several other railway companies and a continuously expanded empire when it bought up several smaller concerns, one of which was the Liverpool, Crosby & Southport Railway, which had initially opened in 1848 and had gone on by 1851 to extend to its full length, with the completion of extensions at each end, to a terminus at Southport Chapel Street in the north and Liverpool Exchange in the south. The L&Y purchased the line in 1855. The route was relatively flat and, when first opened, served areas that were little more than villages. The line followed, for the most part, the coastline, and at the northern end the landscape was dominated by sand dunes. Southport itself had become popular as a tourist destination and latterly a residential district for those wealthy enough to escape the growing congestion that was engulfing Liverpool following the Industrial Revolution. It was this kind of traveller that the line was built to attract. The L&Y continued to expand their empire in the 1850s, and in 1859 they acquired the East Lancashire Railway, which gave them a monopoly of services into Liverpool Exchange.

In the last years of the nineteenth century and first few of the twentieth, the established suburban railways across Britain found themselves facing a new challenge to their dominance of that particular market from street tramways, which had rid themselves of horse power and were starting to adopt the new technology of electric traction. Across many cities, trolley wires were being strung above the streets, and the clip-clop of horses' hooves began to give way to the whine of the faster, more efficient and more frequent electric tramcars. Liverpool and the Wirral

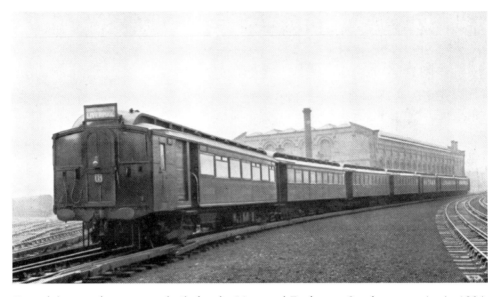

One of the new four-car sets built for the Liverpool Exchange–Southport service in 1904. (Author's Collection)

Peninsula were both to benefit from this development, but the expansion did not affect the L&Y, whose lines out of Liverpool Exchange did not have any serious tramway competition. Nonetheless the L&Y took a very serious look at the benefits of electric traction and how it could enhance their short-distance operations. The General Manager of the L&Y, John Aspinall, had followed the development of electric traction with a professional interest, being an accomplished engineer. He had been the company's Chief Mechanical Engineer from 1886 until taking his current role in 1899. Aspinall looked objectively at the subject, and his opinion was that electrification was the way of the future; not only did the steam locomotives burn coal at a higher price than a power station but the electric multiple unit offered savings in manpower costs and the opportunity to run a faster service at more regular intervals, something the tramways were exploiting at the expense of the main-line railway companies. While the level of competition the L&Y were facing in the area was small at present, new housing developments along the route from Liverpool to Southport would soon be attracting competitors, and the L&Y needed to ensure it stayed ahead of this. He proposed full electrification of the route to the L&Y board in a report of 1902. The board considered the proposal and gave it their blessing, including an extension to the scheme which would see a second route added to the plan. The L&Y had taken over the West Lancashire Railway in 1897, and part of their route from Southport to Crossens, along with the triangle around Meols Cop, was added. The latter location was also to be eventually chosen as the site of the new carriage workshops to service the new electric fleet.

The interior of the L&Y Southport substation, showing the rotary converters used to supply DC current to the conductor rails. (Author's Collection)

The L&Y undertook the construction of a large power station dedicated to supplying the newly electrified lines at Formby. The steam to drive the generators was produced by no fewer than sixteen Lancashire boilers, feeding compound engines that made the generator sets deliver the current to the railway at a pressure of 625 volts DC. Substations were provided at Birkdale, Seaforth and Bank Hall. The power supply to the trains was by the fourth rail system, the same as that employed on the Mersey Railway. All electrical apparatus was supplied to the L&Y under contract by Dick, Kerr & Co. of Preston. This included all of the traction motors and switchgear for the newly built electric multiple units. The trains were built at the L&Y's own workshops at Horwich and Newton Heath. They followed the pattern set by the Mersey Railway in being inspired by American design, despite the fact that this was an entirely British-funded and engineered project. The large saloons featured a mix of transverse and longitudinal seating, with first- and third-class accommodation, the former having upholstered cushions and the latter being merely varnished wooden benches. The trains were made up of four-car units, each vehicle being 60 feet long, with clerestory roofs and mounted on bogies. The two end vehicles were driving motor ones, and had the driving position with a passenger door at the other end; trailers had passenger doors at each end. All the passenger doors were recessed into the vestibule and the early operation was intended to have passengers alight from one end only and boarding passengers join from the other, in an attempt to reduce station dwell times. Gangways were fitted between vehicles, like those that had previously only been seen on longer-distance express stock, allowing passengers to move between cars; this was useful at busier times when empty seats became hard to come by. The cars were steel framed with wooden bodies. The motor coaches had their bodies lined with steel in an attempt to make them more fire resistant, given the high current apparatus that was mounted inside them. A distinctive feature of the vehicles was their width. The Southport line had a very generous loading gauge and as the vehicles were not going to operate on any other route it was decided to exploit this, so the vehicles had a width of 10 feet, making them the widest trains to run in Britain. The wide bodies gave a 2+3 seating arrangement in third class, with a more generous 2+2 in first; a four-car unit formed of motor-trailer-trailer-motor could seat 138 third- and 56 first-class passengers. The electric lighting and heating that was provided throughout meant that passengers on the new service would feel a whole world apart from the gaslit compartment stock that the electric units were to replace. One tradition that the L&Y retained from steam days on their electric stock was the use of the vacuum brake, against the practice followed by other such companies adopting electric traction.

An early L&Y electric service runs in Bootle. Note the boards on the platform advising travellers where the various sections of the train were. (Author's Collection)

Installation of the electrification equipment, and construction of the new works associated with it, was very brisk given the scale of the project. The first test trains were running by late 1903 and on 22 March 1904 the first official electric passenger train ran from Liverpool to Southport and on to Crossens. A few weeks later and the electric trains were sharing the service with the steam ones, while the final deliveries of the new stock were being completed. The full introduction was delayed due to a subsidence at the Formby power station, which was not corrected until May of that year. The electrification was not just a renewal of the train service; it was a reinvention, with a new timetable that offered a train from Liverpool to Southport every twenty minutes and a stopping train that went as far as Hall Road run between them. New stations were built along the route to serve areas that were being built up, and the pace of development of new housing was only increased with the arrival of the new timetable and stations. Another type of vehicle that made its national debut in Britain was the electric baggage car. This was essentially a standard motor car with a cab at each end and no passenger seating inside, the interior being given over to empty space for luggage and other commodities to be carried. Aspinall was rightly proud of his new electric railway and, even before the full service was introduced, had convinced the L&Y board to add another line to the plan. The Southport line electrification was to also be the catalyst for significant improvements to the pioneering LOR.

A train departs Blundellsands station. (Author's Collection)

5

Turn It On

The Liverpool Overhead Railway had met with considerable success upon opening, with the expected traffic of workers, visitors and those on business needing to travel freely between the various docks flocking to it. This was a good start, but the railway knew it had to maximise revenue from other sources if it was to continue to build upon this position. The railway looked at extensions to its line at both ends that would tap into residential markets further out from the dock traffic to do this. The first extension was opened the year after the initial opening of the line and was a quarter of a mile to the north, where a new station was built at Seaforth Sands. At the same time, additional trains were ordered to both cope with the increasing demand and improve the frequency of the service. Lessons had been learned from the initial batch of thirty driving motor coaches and these were incorporated into the second batch of trains. The largest difference was that the length of the cars was shortened to 40 feet in order to better cope with the dynamic forces experienced on the curved sections of the line; otherwise the style and appearance externally was the same. The number of seats remained the same as the first batch, but there was less room for standing passengers. A third batch of trains was ordered to cope with passenger numbers; the number of passenger journeys had risen to nearly 8 million a year. The eight new trains had three carriages, two motor coaches of entirely third-class accommodation and an intermediate trailer, where all the first-class seating was provided. Only eight motor coaches were built, and the remaining four trailers were inserted in the formation between four existing two-car units that were modified to match the new-build ones, which had 70 hp motors to cope with the extra load of the trailer car in the formation. The fleet was constructed and entered service between 1897 and 1898.

The LOR was ready to progress with its next extension, one which it hoped would open up a whole new traffic flow to them. The LOR constructed a new spur from alongside their station at Seaforth Sands and headed north over Crosby Road and onto the Lancashire & Yorkshire Railway station at Seaforth & Litherland, where a physical connection was made with that company's newly electrified

Liverpool Exchange–Southport line. This not only gave the two companies the chance to connect with each other, but went further, in that the possibility existed for trains of one company to run over the metals of the other. While both were DC electric railways it was not as simple as that, and both companies had to make changes or concessions to the needs of the other in order to achieve their common goal. The biggest difference was in the way that electricity was supplied to the trains. The LOR used a centre live rail at 500 volts DC, while the L&Y had the fourth rail system with the live rail outside the track gauge at 625 volts DC. The LOR decided to adopt the L&Y system for not only the extension to its line but the whole of its route and set about laying the new live conductor rails. The original centre live rails were retained and were re-wired to become the new earth return rail; the voltage on the LOR remained at 500 volts DC. The conversion was completed in time for the northern extension to open in 1905. Prior to this in December 1896 the LOR had reached the extent of its southern extension with the line from Herculaneum to Dingle being opened for traffic. Construction of this section had differed considerably from the method used on the rest of the line. The first section from a junction just north of Herculaneum Station was a 250-yard-long girder bridge that crossed over the marshalling yard of the Cheshire Lines. After this the line burrowed under the hillside into a tunnel of over half a mile in length to reach the site of Dingle station. The station was sited in Park Road. It had a brick building on the road itself where the passenger entrance and exit was, but the island terminus platforms were underground, which was totally alien to a railway with the word 'overhead' in its title. The new station was electrically lit, and a ramp down from street level to the platforms was provided, as the depth was not sufficient for lifts to be considered necessary. All of the extra mileage and trains meant the LOR's original power station needed extending and new boilers and dynamos installed alongside the existing ones. The master control board was also replaced with an enlarged version. The LOR must have had great faith in their extensions bringing in new traffic and revenue, as neither had been cheap to build; the Dingle extension alone was a large feat of engineering. On 2 July 1905 it became possible to board a train at Seaforth & Litherland and travel all the way to Dingle. The LOR had reached its maximum length, but its trains would venture further in time.

The L&Y had ambitions to run through services over the LOR using the new direct connection at Seaforth & Litherland. As previously mentioned, they had to make allowances to enable this to happen, as their regular fleet of 60-foot-long trains were too long, too wide and too heavy for the stations and the unique structure on which the LOR ran. In order to get around this, a small fleet of twelve double-ended cars, which were both shorter and lighter than the Southport line cars, was built. These had seats for seventy passengers of both first and third class. The new vehicles were capable of operating in multiple, and were run as single, double or on rare occasions three-car sets. The Dingle Cars, as they became

Three-car working became the norm on the LOR by 1914. Here is one of the three-car sets that subsequently had their bodies widened to hold even more passengers, pictured at Hushisson station in 1956. (Jim Peden)

The lattice girder bridge that spanned the Cheshire Lines Committee yard at Herculaneum, and carried the LOR's southern extension into Dingle tunnel. (Jim Peden)

known, were fully compatible with the rest of the L&Y operation, and could be used elsewhere on the L&Y Merseyside electric network.

Linking up with the LOR was not the only ambition the L&Y had for extending their electric services. The board had approved a scheme that would see conductor rails laid between Sandhills and Ormskirk, so that an electric service could be run from there to Liverpool Exchange. The work began with the equipping of the section from Sandhills to Aintree in November 1906, and the remainder was added in sections until Ormskirk was switched on in April 1913. In addition, the North Mersey branch between Marsh Lane Junction and Aintree was added to the scheme, with two new stations built along the route at Ford and Linacre Road; the last section to be added was the spur from North Mersey Junction to Gladstone Dock, which went live in 1914. To operate these additional routes, the L&Y had extra carriages built to supplement their existing fleet. The opening up of the route to Aintree to electric traction gave the LOR the chance to run services there for the larger race meetings. This included the Grand National and Jump Sunday. The LOR trains had been built to operate at a maximum of 500 volts DC so had to be limited to series-only operation on the L&Y metals, which were energised at 625 volts DC. This practice continued up until the closure of the LOR.

By the time of the outbreak of the First World War, Merseyside could boast no fewer than three companies offering electric commuter services into and around the city of Liverpool, two of which were physically linked and integrated in their service provision. In terms of mileage of electrified track, only London and Newcastle were in a position to rival the area, and the city was at the forefront of a rail transport revolution that showed no sign of slowing down. The passengers appreciated the cleaner electric trains, which were a world apart from the gaslit carriages that less than two decades earlier had been the norm. The clock face timetable, reasonable fares policy and quick journey times electrification offered gave rise to something called 'The Sparks Effect', whereby lines that were served by electric railways became targets for new housing developments and resulted in an increase in commuter patronage, as they were simply far more efficient than the steam lines. The L&Y knew they had been taken in the right direction by Aspinall to adopt the new power for their Merseyside operation, and now turned their thoughts to the other major city in the empire; Manchester was ready for the Sparks Effect.

The brick-built exterior of Dingle station, where passengers went underground to board an 'overhead' train. (Author's Collection)

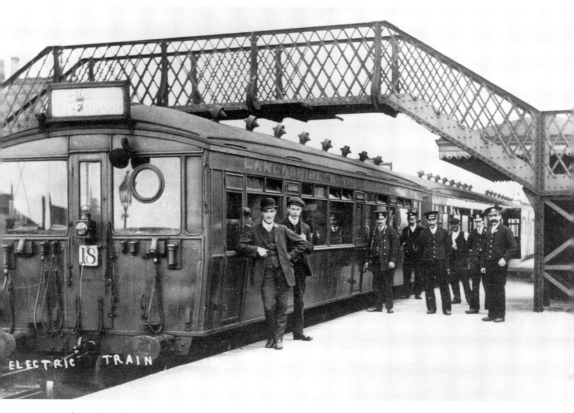

A posed L&Y publicity shot showing staff and the Dingle cars. The picture was taken after the L&Y ceased regular operations over the LOR, and is believed to be at Maghull in October 1910. (Author's Collection)

6

Dreams Are All We Have

Manchester had been little more than a reasonably sized market town in the early eighteenth century. Then the Industrial Revolution happened in and around the town, and the place was never going to be the same again. Mechanised industry arrived, with the promise of regular employment, prosperity and a new life for thousands of ordinary people, who were drawn to the new factories from the rural areas. The population quite literally exploded in a matter of years, and the town grew into a city to such an extent that it burst at the seams. Previously rural areas were swallowed up in the expansion and became suburbs of the North West's great industrial capital. Housing began to be in short supply, and living conditions for the humble factory worker sank to a frighteningly poor standard, with disease, poor sanitation and infant mortality rife. Against this backdrop, the middle and merchant classes made their escape from the squalor and headed for the newer, and less densely populated, outer suburban areas. At first these were to the south of the city, but in time the migration became more adventurous, helped in no small measure by the arrival of the railways in the middle of the nineteenth century. One such railway line that contributed to this was the East Lancashire Railway, which had opened as far as Bury, to the north of the city, in 1846. In time this line was to expand considerably to serve other districts and towns in the west of the county. By 1859 the company had merged into the expanding empire of the Lancashire & Yorkshire Railway, whose head offices were in Manchester. The L&Y had completed the electrification of some of their lines out of Liverpool and were convinced of the benefits that electric traction could bring to suburban rail travel; and of course the economies that it would also bring to their balance sheets. The factors driving them to look at electrification in Manchester were the same as those forcing other companies to do the same in various other metropolitan areas during the first decade of the twentieth century, namely rising coal prices, increased competition from electrified tramways and a need to streamline their operations and reduce the traffic flows around terminus stations. Electrification offered the latter in the form of the electrical multiple unit, which could enter and leave a terminus station without the need for a second locomotive and crew to be provided. EMUs did not need coal stages, water towers or two employees on the footplate. They were cleaner, faster and enabled a timetable to be run with departures at the same minutes past each hour, as the train was always ready to leave, being freed from the routine of replenishing coal and water. The biggest drawback to electrification was a significant one, however; the infrastructure and rolling stock fleets needed huge initial investment from the outset, and while this could be recovered from the savings already mentioned, it did oblige the company to pay up front in the hope of reaping a longer-term reward.

The Lancashire & Yorkshire Railway should be applauded for their forward-thinking in terms of railway electrification; they were one of the first major companies to adopt the method of working, and were making an obvious investment in the future of their traffic, which stemmed from both a confidence in the service they could offer and a belief that electric traction was a power of the future, and not simply a passing technology that would be bettered within a few years by some other new discovery. The rise in railway electrification at this time was not just confined to Britain but was being seen across the globe; indeed, by comparison it could be argued that Britain was very slow off the mark compared to America, Switzerland, Germany, France and many other nations. It was against this backdrop of global expansion that British firms were competing for exports, and one such company was Dick, Kerr & Co. Ltd of Preston, who had supplied the L&Y for their Southport line electrification. They were seeking to break into export markets and were looking for an opportunity to demonstrate the new products they could offer the global customer base. It was through a partnership with the L&Y that the first electrified lines around Manchester came into being.

The 3¾-mile-long branch line from Bury Bolton Street to Holcombe Brook was a former East Lancashire Railway line that had been absorbed into the L&Y. In isolation it did not feature as a high-level candidate for electrification, being simply regarded as a feeder route for traffic on the Manchester Victoria–Bury route, which was being considered for electrification by the L&Y. Dick, Kerr & Co. were looking for a line upon which they could install a high-voltage DC electrification system that could be used as a demonstrator in the hope of winning a large export order for Brazil, and in time other overseas customers. The route was electrified with overhead wires energised at 3,600 volts DC. Overhead wires had been used as a power supply in the UK before, but on the AC systems that were operated by both the Midland and London, Brighton & South Coast railways. This was to be the first use of a high-voltage DC overhead wire in the world. Two trains were built to operate the passenger service at the L&Y works at Newton Heath. They followed the outline of the second batch of stock built for the Merseyside lines, with elliptical roofs replacing the American-influenced clerestories and open saloon passenger accommodation with driving cabs at the outer ends, which also featured gangways, so when coupled to another unit passengers could walk the entire length of the train. The motor coaches had a pantograph for current collection on each end,

A Dick, Kerr & Co. publicity shot of the experimental 3,600-volt DC overhead electrification work carried out on the Holcombe Brook line. (Author's Collection)

and on these vehicles each axle had a 250 hp nose-suspended traction motor. The high-voltage DC supply meant that the low voltage needed to operate the trains' control gear had to be supplied at 120 volts DC from a small rotary transformer also mounted under the floor of the motor coaches. A ten-minute interval service on the line could be maintained by the use of only one set, which was more than adequate to meet traffic demands. To supply electricity to the overhead wires, a substation at Holcombe Brook was constructed. Following trials and crew training the new electric service commenced public operation in July 1913. While the trial was considered a success, there were no direct contracts won by Dick, Kerr & Co. from it.

In 1915 the L&Y were pushing on with their own plans for the electrification of the trunk route to Bury from Manchester Victoria. The works were authorised in December 1913, with Dick, Kerr & Co. again being the contractors for the supply of the traction equipment for the trains and the power station that was to be built at Clifton. This site was chosen due to a ready supply of water for cooling and easy access for coal trains to feed the boilers, which fed steam to two 5,000-kW turbo-alternating sets; these produced 6,600-volt AC electricity that was sent to substations at Manchester Victoria and Radcliffe then converted to 1,200 volts DC. Unlike the Southport line, the current was supplied to the trains by an unusual side-contact third rail that remained a unique feature of the line up until the early 1990s. The conductor rails were made for the L&Y by a contractor in Stoke, and were placed on glass insulators outside the track gauge. The live rail was further screened from potential contact by persons on the line by vertical wooden boards. The negative return was achieved through the running rails. The collector shoe was mounted on a beam on both bogies of a motor coach, and sprung loaded so it pressed out and against the side of the live rail. As mentioned, this was an arrangement unique to this line and not, to the best of my knowledge, found anywhere else in Europe. The only obvious benefit of the layout was that it was only slightly less prone to bad conductivity in the winter in the event of a build-up of snow or ice, as the contact surface of the conductor rail was better shielded from the elements than the top contact ones of the other railways using conductor rails. Of course the overhead wires on the Holcombe Brook branch were immune to the weather and this was to become one of the factors that made this method of electrification more appealing to future generations of engineers.

To operate the intensive service on the 22-mile-long route to Bury, the L&Y had a fleet of EMUs built at their Horwich works, and they introduced a few advances in EMU design. The vehicles were of all-metal construction, with steel being used for the frames and aluminium for the body panels. The outward appearance bore a resemblance to the Holcombe Brook units, and inside the seating was in open-plan saloons with through gangways over the length of the train achieved by vestibules on the ends of both driving and non-driving coaches. The trains were marshalled into five-coach formations with a driving motor at each end and in the middle, with

The layout of running and conductor rails on the L&Y Manchester–Bury route, showing the wooden boards protecting the conductor rail. (Author's Collection)

two trailer cars in the second and fourth position. The units carried multiple unit jumpers on each cab end, and had automatic couplers, so the formation was not fixed and could be amended as traffic requirements and stock availability dictated. Two of the five vehicles were for first-class passengers, which was popular among the many business travellers using the route. The interior of these cars had carpets, and the seats were generously upholstered. The remaining three coaches, provided for third-class passengers, had seating for 106 people on basic rattan-covered seats. All heating and lighting was electrically powered from the traction supply, and unlike the Southport line stock the Manchester-area trains all used air brakes. The vehicles were heavier than previous builds, due in part to their all-metal construction, with a motor coach weighing in at 54 tons compared to the 29 tons of the trailer cars. Each motor coach had four 200 hp nose-suspended traction motors and enabled a five-car train to cover the route in twenty-four minutes as opposed to the thirty-two minutes taken by the steam trains they replaced.

The full introduction of the electric trains on the Manchester Victoria–Bury route was delayed by the outbreak of the First World War. The first few services running on the steam timetable began to appear from April 1916, and in the summer the whole timetable was revised when the full electric service commenced. The L&Y had continued to operate the Holcombe Brook line as a shuttle service using the high-voltage DC equipment supplied by Dick, Kerr & Co., but had decided to standardise it alongside the new service, so the L&Y bought the equipment from the contractor and then set about dismantling it and converting the line to the same side-contact 1,200 volts DC. This was completed during 1918, and the branch

Interior of one of the substations on the Bury route. (Author's Collection)

A photograph showing the arrangement of shoe beam and current collector shoe on the Manchester–Bury units. (Author's Collection)

became part of the L&Y Manchester electric network, using stock from the main route. The two overhead units were at first placed into store, and then in 1927 converted into an experimental diesel-electric unit, which was not a success and fell out of use quickly before going for scrap.

By the end of hostilities in 1918 the electric railways of the North West were established and proving popular. This went against the grain for Britain's railways, which had been created from dozens of separate companies, often competing against each other, and now with the economy battered from four years of 'total war' the industry was fast entering decline. Action had to be taken to arrest this and get the railways back to their role of providing essential, reliable, affordable and regular transport for post-war Britain.

7

Day of the Lords

The biggest shake-up of Britain's railways since their creation occurred in 1921, when the Railway Act was put before Parliament. During the First World War the railways were seen as essential for the war effort and had been placed under government control. This lasted until 1921 and had resulted in the system becoming largely rundown and worn out in many parts, so strong and focussed leadership was needed to rebuild it. The post-war government, led by Prime Minister David Lloyd George, and his Minister for Transport, Eric Campbell Geddes, recognised that the 120 separate companies that currently ran their own empires of varying sizes would not be up to this challenge and there was too much competition and far too little cooperation. Their proposals to end this set-up had stopped short of full-scale nationalisation of the network, but they intended to take drastic action to end the current impasse and amalgamate over 100 companies into just four. The White Paper for the Act was published in 1920 and met with fierce opposition from the railway companies themselves. The L&Y had taken action to end competition in their part of the system by merging with their largest competitor, the London & North Western Railway, in 1922. Despite the opposition, the Bill was passed by Parliament and took effect from 1 January 1923, becoming known as the Railway Grouping. There were a number of lines that were exempt from the provisions of the legislation as they were either run by joint committees or were isolated lines that offered very specific services and had no direct competition from other railways; two such examples of the latter were the Liverpool Overhead Railway and the Mersey Railway, who both continued to operate beyond the Grouping just as they had before it. With the exception of those two lines that remained independent, the former L&Y lines were now under the management of a much larger company, the London Midland & Scottish Railway (LMS), who had responsibility for nearly all services from London Euston to the Midlands, North West, Cumbria and large parts of Scotland. On the opposite side of the country, the London & North Eastern Railway (LNER) operated all the services from King's Cross to Yorkshire, the North East, the eastern side of Scotland and the former Great Eastern lines from London to Essex and East Anglia. The Southern Railway were running everything from London to the South Coast, and the last of the 'Big Four' was the Great Western Railway (GWR), who operated out of Paddington to Wales and the West Country.

At the time of the Grouping, railway electrification was one area of the industry that was seen as promoting traffic growth. The problem was that all of the different companies who had adopted it in some form had done so with little thought for standardisation. The North West boasted four differing systems with third- and fourth-rail DC of 500 volts DC (LOR), 600 volts DC (Mersey Railway), 625 volts DC (L&Y Merseyside) and 1,200 volts DC side contact (L&Y Manchester). In addition there were other parts of the country where third and fourth rail was operated at different voltages, while in addition the North Eastern Railway had taken up the challenge of overhead wires with a system operating at 1,500 volts DC and had ambitions to electrify their York–Edinburgh main line with it. Elsewhere, both the London, Brighton & South Coast and Midland railways were also using overhead wires, but conducting electric power of AC current (of which more later). The government set up a committee to look at the issue in 1921, when the Railways Act was being debated. This was followed in 1927 by a government committee chaired by Sir John Pringle, then the Chief Inspecting Officer of Railways. Among its remits was to evaluate and decide which methods of electrification were the best in practice, not only from within the UK but overseas too, to allow for economic installation and the interchange of locomotives and rolling stock. The report of the committee was published July 1928 and recommended that there be two standard voltages, 1,500 volts DC overhead wire and 750 volts DC third rail, with an exception given to underground lines, where a fourth rail was required for negative return as it had better insulation in that environment. The report went on to say that locomotives should be equipped for both methods of current collection where through running was envisaged, and gave the distances and heights at which conductor rails and overhead wires should be placed in relation to the running rails, recommending that these be standard across all companies – however, this should only be enforced by a company when it had replaced one-third of its motive power with electrically driven machines. The Pringle report was a step in the right direction, but even the 'Big Four' companies were not bound to modify their existing infrastructure based upon its recommendations, and only new or renewed projects were obliged to adopt the new standards.

Another significant piece of legislation that impacted on not only railway electrification but the use of electricity in homes and workplaces was the Electricity (Supply) Act of 1926. Within that Bill were laid the foundations for our present-day national grid and the creation of the Central Electricity Board, which standardised the supply of domestic power in Britain. Prior to the Act there were some 600 companies supplying power at different voltages; some were AC while there were a few offering the DC system. After the Act was passed, they all had to feed AC power at 50 cycles a second (Hertz) into their local grids, which covered most

RAILWAY ELECTRIFICATION COMMITTEE, 1927.

Drawing Nº 4.

STANDARDISATION OF CONTACT RAILS

DIAGRAM ILLUSTRATING RECOMMENDATIONS RELATIVE TO THE POSITION OF CONTACT SURFACES AND CLEARANCES OF CONTACT RAIL AND SHOE CONSTRUCTION.

— TOP CONTACT RAIL —
Ref para: H(I)-(i), (ii), (iii).

Contact surface
Rail
1'-4"
Plane of top table of track rails
₵ of contact surfaces
Gauge line of Track

— UNDER CONTACT RAIL —
Ref. para: H (I)-(i), (ii), (iii), (vi)

Limit of construction not less than 1'-1½"
Rail
1'-4"
Plane of top table of track rails
Contact surface
Limit of construction not less than 1'-7½"

— CLEARANCE BELOW SHOES IN FREE POSITION —
Ref. para: H(I)-(i), (ii), (vii)

Not less than
Shoe
1'-4"
Plane of top table of track rails

One of the drawings issued under the 1927 Pringle report, showing the dimensions for the 'standardisation' of conductor rail installation. (Crown Copyright)

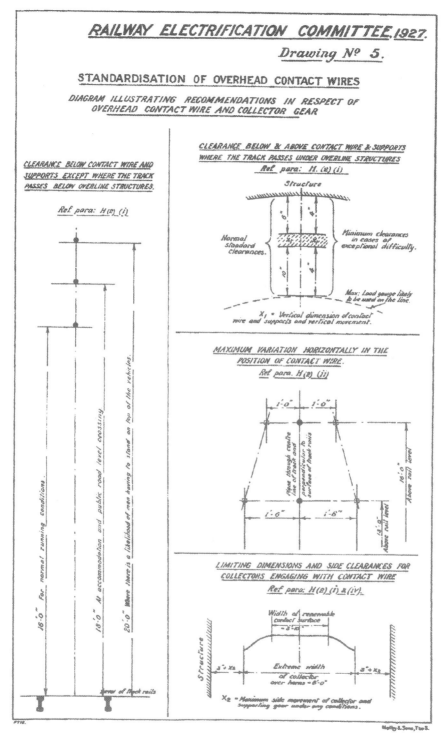

Another of the drawings from the Pringle report. This one sets out the standards for placement and clearance regarding overhead wires. (Crown Copyright)

of the country, and one area could be used to back up another as they were all working to the same standard. The impact of this on the railways was that future schemes would no longer have to rely on building their own power stations, as there was a ready supply from outside sources that they could tap into for their specific use.

Parliament was not yet done with the subject of electricity and its application to rail. A new committee was set up September 1929 under the chairmanship of Lord Weir of Eastwood to examine further the question of main-line electrification in view of the progress being made with the widespread availability of high-tension electricity supply. The Weir committee looked at the financial justification for further investment in electrification, and concluded that there was little financial gain to be made from widespread electrification compared to existing fuel costs, and that the bulk of the savings that a conversion to electric traction offered was in reduced manpower costs, infrastructure savings, such as removing the need for turntables, and the time steam locomotives stand idle or being prepared for service compared to their electric cousins. The report concluded that main-line electrification in Britain had certain benefits and should be continued with, but only where there was a strong financial case for it; the greater use of electricity by the railways would also lead to better supply being provided by the electricity companies, and this would benefit urban and rural domestic users. Weir's committee went on to further endorse the standards for conductor rails and overhead wires made by the Pringle report without any modification. The report also recognised that the railways were now facing another growing competitor to their trade, the domestic car. All of this will appear blatantly obvious to the average student of railways looking at the report with the benefit of over eighty years of experience of railway electrification, but that level of experience was non-existent in 1931 and electrification was handled with care due to its high investment and long-term-benefit business model. The industry had worked with steam as its prime mover for a hundred years, and any attempt to stray away from that was bound to meet with suspicion; hard evidence was going to be needed to change that mindset.

Following the establishment of the 'Big Four' and all of the legislation and reports that had followed, it was certain that further electrification would take place, but no government money was going to be made available for it. The railway companies would have to fund any future projects from their own purses. There would be a definite change of appearance and feel from those earlier schemes for schemes that took place post-Grouping. While there were those within the upper echelons of the industry that resented all the 'meddling from Whitehall', it is fair to say with decades of hindsight that the plans for standardisation, based upon the technology that existed at the time, were certainly prudent and well intended. The stage was now set for the next big projects to get under way in the north-west of England.

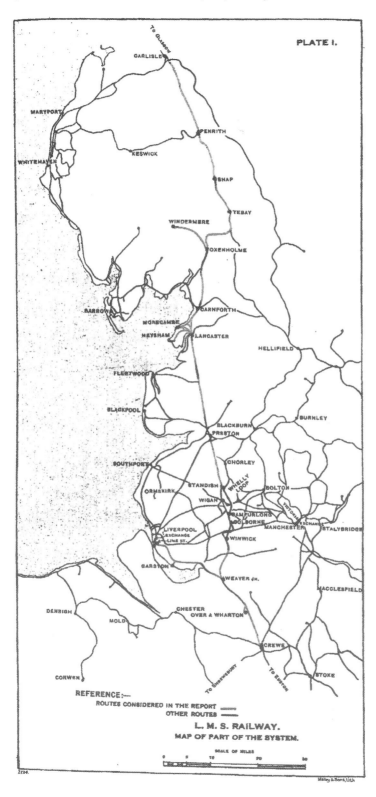

Map of the LMS
lines considered
under the 1931 Weir
committee. The lines
in light grey were
considered for main-
line electrification.
As can be seen, these
included both the
route to Liverpool
Lime Street and
north from Weaver
Junction to Glasgow.
Manchester was not
under consideration
by the report.
(Crown Copyright)

8

Up in the Sky

Altrincham is a market town 8 miles south-west from Manchester city centre. At the start of the nineteenth century it could boast a population of just over 1,500. By 1849 the population had nearly trebled and this was in no small part due to the arrival of both cotton mills and the railway. The latter was the Manchester South Junction & Altrincham Railway (MSJ&A), opened in 1849 from London Road station in the city, which followed a route of just over 13 miles via Old Trafford, Sale and Timperley to reach the town. The railway passed through areas that were slow to develop in Victorian times but that had changed by the start of the twentieth century, and the route had a strong base of commuting clientele, a fact that attracted stiff competition from the electric tramways and eroded the line's patronage to the extent that action needed to be taken. The MSJ&A had an unusual management arrangement, as it was owned jointly by two railway companies: the London & North Western Railway and the Manchester, Sheffield & Lincolnshire Railway. At the time of the Grouping, the former became a part of the LMS while the latter was now a part of the LNER, which left the MSJ&A as one of a handful of lines that was jointly owned by two of the 'Big Four' and had to be run by a management committee with representatives of both railways. Prior to the Grouping, the line's joint owners had seriously considered an electrification scheme but failed to act upon it. The matter was revisited in the late 1920s and this time the joint committee that managed the line authorised work to commence with an estimated cost of £500,000.

In keeping with the recommendations of the Pringle report the system chosen was 1,500 volts DC overhead wires, something the LNER were keen to experiment with, but it would be the LMS who took the lead on this project, with responsibility for not only the installation of the masts, wires and substations but the construction of the rolling stock too. In 1927 the LMS had introduced a standard pattern for their new electric stock that could only be described as a backward step. Given that one of their constituent companies had started building all-steel cars before the First World War, it is a mystery why the LMS adopted the steam stock practice of steel underframe, and wooden body frame overlaid with steel panels for their new design. Gone too were the spacious open saloons of the American-influenced cars and their more British outline successors, and back were the full-width closed-in compartments. It is fair to say that these carriages were near identical to what was being provided on steam-hauled commuter routes; the only concession to electric traction was the provision of electric lighting and heating from the line voltage supply and the absence of a tank engine at the front of the train. The first units of this style were built for the fourth-rail-equipped Euston–Watford route in 1927, and were formed of a driving motor car with four Metropolitan Vickers traction motors of 265 hp each. The other vehicles were an intermediate trailer which had both first- and third-class compartments and a driving trailer; the latter car, like the driving motor, had a driving cab at the outer end, with a guard's brake van immediately behind it. A second smaller batch of these units was built for the LMS lines on Merseyside to Southport and Ormskirk, where they earned the nickname of Lindberghs after the *Spirit of St Louis* pilot who made the world's first non-stop transatlantic air crossing in 1927. They were not popular with passengers for the reasons already given, but that did not stop the LMS from using the design for their MSJ&A units. Twenty-two three-car sets were constructed; like the previous units, the work was subcontracted out to Metro Cammell at their works in Wednesbury. The changes needed to the design for overhead line operation were the obvious provision of a pantograph over the cab and brake van end of the motor coach and the much larger traction motors, due to the higher operating voltage. The MSJ&A units had the largest DC traction motor ever fitted to a British EMU, with one 328 hp motor mounted on each axle of the motor coaches. The motors were rated to take 750 volts DC each, so were permanently coupled in series pairs, with the combined motor load capable of utilising the 1,500 volts DC traction supply. The vehicles had standard screw couplings and buffers so they could be towed away from the electrified area by conventional locomotives, but the air brakes were not compatible with the steam locomotives of the time. Total seating capacity for a three-car unit when built was 228 third class and 40 first class. The trains had a top speed of 60 mph, but would rarely have got the chance to achieve this on the line, with its frequent station stops.

In addition to the trains there was the question of the electrification equipment. The power for the line was supplied from the domestic grid, with substations provided at Old Trafford and Timperley. The control room that monitored supply was at the former, with Timperley being operated under remote control. The 11 kV AC supplied by the electricity grid was converted to 1,500 volts DC by rotary converters, and additionally at Old Trafford there was a mercury arc rectifier, the first such use of this device for railway traction in Britain. The overhead wires were suspended from lattice girder structures, and the live wire itself was suspended from these at an average height of 16 feet above the ballast, which had been the standard set by the Pringle report. The train's pantograph was held aloft by compressed air, which was provided from the onboard compressor

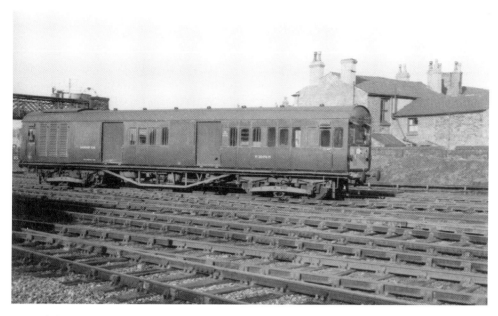

One of the LMS-designed baggage cars, built in 1927 for the Southport and Ormskirk lines, pictured near the end of its life in 1964. (Jim Peden)

A pair of MSJ&A trailer cars are preserved at the Midland Railway Centre. This is one of them in 2014, with the sheet metal skin removed, showing the timber framework of the body. (Graeme Gleaves)

that also fed the braking system. This presented the problem that the pantograph would lower when the train ran out of air were the current to fail for a long period, and in order to get it to raise again a handpump was fitted in the guard's brake to produce enough air to achieve this.

Training for the new service took place on test runs arranged on Sundays, when the line was less active, and on weekdays when trains could be slotted between the steam service. Drivers received a classroom-based training package on the theories of electric traction and the layout of the train before learning to handle the new units. The difference in performance from a steam locomotive was very noticeable; firstly the electric unit was far quicker off the mark and this reduced the overall journey time from Manchester London Road to Altrincham from twenty-seven to twenty-two minutes, and that included three extra stops for the new stations at Warwick Road, Dane Road and Navigation Road. The electrification works also included improvements to signalling and a new depot for stabling the electric

The MSJ&A stock was little altered into BR days. This is M28588M at Altrincham on 9 January 1970. (Basil Hancock)

fleet at Bowdon, with overhead cranes and inspection pits provided so that all the servicing needs of the fleet could be met in house, reducing the need to move units to major workshops for servicing. There were a few additional sidings electrified to enable parts of the fleet to be out-stabled for start- and end-of-service unit diagrams. Testing continued while the finishing touches were put to stations, signalling and the new depot. The full electric service was not introduced progressively but in one overnight change, as had been the case with the Mersey Railway nearly three decades earlier. On Monday 11 May 1931 the new timetable was brought into effect, not without a few teething problems it should be noted, but these were quickly ironed out, and the revised service received critical acclaim from customers and the local media alike, who campaigned for more lines in the area to be likewise electrified. Alas it was not to be, and no further 1,500 volts DC electrifications would be carried out until after the war.

9

Red Frame/White Light

After the railway Grouping the only lines to see any real changes to their daily lives were the former L&Y lines out of Liverpool Exchange. At first this change was visible from the altered train livery, the maroon of the LMS. On the LOR and Mersey Railway, life continued as it had done since the start of their electric services. The LOR had removed their centre negative rails and were operating on the simplified third-rail system; through running of LMS trains over LOR routes had ceased after only a few years, and those passengers that wanted to access the dock estate line at Seaforth & Litherland simply had to change from the LMS to the LOR train there. As the 1920s gave way to the 1930s the world became a harsher place, with a steep economic downturn resulting in high unemployment. While this affected the passenger numbers using the railways it was the policy of the government of the day to use industries like them to stimulate employment and thus the economy back into growth. In 1935 private companies were given the chance to borrow capital from the Treasury at a much reduced rate of interest on the condition that the funds were used for new works and not to prop up ailing concerns. Many railway companies took up the offer to push through projects that would otherwise have remained shelved due to the lack of investment capital that was around at the time. The LMS was one such forward-thinking business, and hatched a scheme that would see them enter into a partnership with the independent Mersey Railway and electrify the lines they operated on the Wirral Peninsula and obtain through running into Liverpool via the Mersey. Such an arrangement was of mutual benefit. By removing the need to change trains at Birkenhead Park station, passengers travelling from stations on the West Kirby and New Brighton branches could use one service to get straight into the city. Such a convenience could only attract higher patronage and increase revenue. There was one obstacle to overcome. The Mersey Railway were unwilling to change their method of working from fourth to third rail, as the bulk of their line was in a tunnel, where the isolated negative return was considered a far superior system to the alternative of returning the negative current through the running rails; in the latter arrangement there is the increased risk of earth leakage, making the traction supply vulnerable to short circuits and loss of current. The LMS scheme was to use the Pringle report standard third rail at a pressure of 650 volts DC, so a means of enabling trains to use both systems was needed; the solution was fiendishly simple. When a train ran from the LMS network onto that of the Mersey Railway, it passed over a magnet in the track that closed a contactor under the train. This rerouted the negative return circuit away from the running rails and into a fourth-rail return shoe mounted under each motor bogie. In the reverse direction the opposite applied, with the magnet opening the contactor and restoring negative return to the running rails. The system was fully automatic and reliable and had to be fitted to the new LMS stock as well as the existing fleet of the Mersey. The Mersey did have to make one significant concession to the LMS electrification, as the conductor rails north of Birkenhead Park were being laid to the standards outlined in the Pringle report and thus were a different distance away from the adjacent running rail from the 1903-installed ones of the older system. The Mersey Railway had to undertake a lengthy programme of resiting their conductor rails to match those of the LMS. This had to be done in sections and at night, resulting in a network with differing conductor rail positions for several weeks. To overcome this without disruption to the service, the Mersey cars were fitted with an additional set of collector shoes to allow them to work normally irrespective of whether they were running over a new or old conductor rail alignment.

The LMS had previously offered a very retrograde, unimaginative unit as its standard design, but they went from one extreme to the other in their choice of unit for the Wirral electrification. The nineteen three-car sets were to be the most futuristic and modern electric units running outside of London, and shared many characteristics with the latest designs running under the capital's streets. The nature of the operation, with tunnels and curves, dictated that the vehicles be slightly lower and narrower than standard, and the driving cars were on 58-foot frames, with the centre trailers slightly shorter, on 56-foot ones. The bodies were all steel, with use made of light alloys and hollow girder frames to reduce weight without compromising the strength of the body shell. The seating was arranged into 2+2 transverse in third class, and just over half the centre trailer was 2+1 first-class accommodation. The passenger doors were sliding air-operated ones with two pairs on either side of each vehicle. The door pockets into which the opening doors slid and which housed the pneumatic pistons that operated them were utilised with longitudinal bench seats, which had the added bonus of increasing standing room around the doorways, a useful feature at heavily loaded peak periods; leather hang straps were provided for standing passengers in these areas. The interiors were all open saloon; each carriage had three areas of seating, with the passenger doors breaking them up; hand-operated sliding doors gave first class an added air of exclusivity, shutting the seated areas off from the door openings. Lighting and heating was all electric with under-seat heaters and tungsten bulbs in opaque ceramic lampshades. The windows were large and had sliding ventilators to allow air in when the interior became stuffy or too hot in the summer. No provision was made for gangway connections between vehicles, and even the guard's compartment at the rear of the driving motor coach was full width, but closed off from the passenger saloon. Under the floor were mounted four 135 hp traction motors, which along with the associated control equipment were supplied by British Thompson Houston of Rugby; one motor was mounted on each axle of the driving motor coach, with the other two vehicles being unpowered trailers. For the first time outside of the London Underground, a train was fitted with two types of brake. Firstly there was the normal Westinghouse-type air brake, which was the fail-safe safety feature. Additionally there was the electro-pneumatic brake, which allowed the driver to 'inject' air directly from the train's reservoirs into the brake cylinders, where it made for faster stopping; the electro-pneumatic brake also allowed for subtle graduated applications or releases to ensure the stop was as smooth as the skill of the person operating it. The trains were finished in the LMS maroon with gold lettering, number and the company crest midway down the lower bodyside of the driving motor coaches. Construction of all the driving motor brake coaches was carried out by Metro Cammell, with the Birmingham Railway Carriage & Wagon Co. at Smethwick building the driving trailers. The construction of the intermediate trailers was split between the two, with ten built by Metro Cammell and nine by the BRC&W Co.

As the Mersey railwaymen had done nearly three and a half decades earlier, the LMS drivers attended a training school set up at Birkenhead North, which was the site of the new maintenance depot for the fleet, to be taught about the new art of electric traction. They also had to learn the routes of the Mersey Railway, and the

A Mersey Railway unit converted to operate on third rail is pictured in 1946. (Author's Collection)

Mersey crews did the same for the LMS routes. The Mersey fleet was much older, despite the additional vehicles (without clerestory roofs) that had been added in batches in the 1920s, and had been built with only the short journey times of the Mersey Railway in mind. As such they had no heaters and their brake reservoirs were replenished at each end of the original line. Neither arrangement would be suitable in the age of through working, so the older fleet had to go through a facelift, with the interiors spruced up, electric heating fitted and air compressors installed on the motor coaches to supply the train's braking system.

The changeover to all electric working on the Wirral and Mersey lines took place on Sunday 13 March 1938 with the switching-on ceremony conducted by Joshua Stamp, the president of the LMS, who had arrived on a ceremonial last steam train. From that day on, LMS trains worked directly from either New Brighton or West Kirby to Liverpool Central or from Liverpool to Rock Ferry, where the Mersey Railway connected with the GWR routes south towards Chester. The Mersey Railway trains were able to do the same, and the frequency of service on all routes increased markedly. Patronage rose directly as a result, with more residents of the Wirral lines choosing to commute direct to Liverpool by train.

While the modernisation and electrification of the Wirral lines was being completed, the LMS turned their attention to the Southport and Ormskirk lines in particular. The original stock was now over thirty-five years old and was starting to show its age. With the arrival of the modern trains being built for the Wirral, these venerable old L&Y units would only be made to look even older. The LMS decided to replace the whole fleet with a new design that was not dissimilar to those entering service on the Wirral lines. The new Southport line fleet was much bigger due to the generous loading gauge of that line, with 2+3 seating in third class and 2+2 in first. Fifty-nine units were built, formed of thirty-four three-car sets and twenty-five two cars. The three cars had a driving motor coach with English Electric supplied traction equipment; this kept with the old L&Y tradition as the English Electric Company had been formed of an amalgamation of engineering concerns which included the original supplier to the L&Y, Dick, Kerr & Co. The traction motors on each axle were 230 hp each and just like the Wirral stock all axles ran in roller bearings with electro-pneumatic brakes and contactors for switching through the resistances for acceleration. The L&Y lines had been converted to third rail only several years before so the new units were built to operate only on this system. The new trains had a top speed of 70 mph but this was guesswork as no speedometer was provided in the cab! Construction of the vehicles was undertaken at the LMS carriage works in Derby and like the Wirral stock the LMS livery of maroon was applied.

The re-equipping of the Southport line took place at the start of the Second World War, with the last cars not being delivered until 1941. Liverpool was tactically a hugely significant area to the war effort with the Royal Navy having a large presence on the river, with their corvettes and frigates based there to undertake

The two driving motor coaches of the LMS Wirral stock made spare by enemy action are pictured in Birkenhead North shed after the end of the war, wearing British Railways crests. (Jim Peden)

An as-built LMS Southport unit at Chapel Street station. (Author's Collection)

An early publicity photograph of the LMS-built stock for the Southport line. This was probably taken after 1945 due to wartime restrictions on photography. (Author's Collection)

anti-submarine duties to protect the Atlantic shipping convoys. The Mersey docks were the intended destination of many of those convoys. The significance of the city was not lost on the enemy and Liverpool became the second most bombed city after London. Travelling around the city by rail during blackout conditions became hazardous even when there wasn't an air raid with the trains exhibiting minimal lighting to hide their presence from the Luftwaffe. The LOR, due to its location adjacent to the docks, was in the front line of the bombing campaign and the structure along with several of its stations suffered various direct hits, putting sections of the line out of action for weeks while the line was repaired; amazingly the LOR never lost a single one of its trains to enemy action. The same could not be said of the LMS with the docks at Birkenhead also being a focus of air raids. The new Wirral line depot at Birkenhead North took a direct hit in 1940 and the two relatively new units stabled inside were so badly damaged that only the driving motor coaches could be recovered. This left the fleet short and the spare vehicles were stored in the shed for several years until replacement vehicles could be built in the 1950s. The Mersey Railway also lost vehicles when Liverpool Central and Birkenhead Park stations were bombed. Despite all of this the electric railways continued to operate to the best of their abilities throughout the duration with temporary patch repairs being made to the infrastructure to keep the traffic flowing. Such was the importance of the Mersey electric lines that as a contingency

The interior of the driving cab of an LMS Southport line unit. The earlier built Wirral units had a near identical cab layout. (Author's Collection)

After nationalisation, and wearing BR green livery, but still in as-built condition, an LMS-built Southport line unit passes Birkdale on 15 March 1963, bound for Liverpool Exchange. (Jim Peden)

measure four old trains of Hammersmith & City line stock that had been made redundant by replacement stock were refurbished and sent north for storage at Hoylake and Birkenhead North as a contingency should any further LMS or Mersey Railway units be lost. In the event they were never called upon and ended up being towed away for scrap in 1945.

By the end of hostilities in 1945, as had been the case at the end of the previous war, all of Britain's railways were battered, both financially and physically. They could be proud of the contribution they made to the war effort but once again Parliament would need to take action to save them from collapse in the new post-war Britain.

10

There Goes the Fear

The LNER had been the sleeping partner in the MSJ&A electrification of 1931. They had been a business partner as one of the line's joint owners but had left the leadership of the scheme's engineering to the LMS. This was surprising given that one of the constituent companies of the LNER at the grouping had been the North Eastern Railway who, under the guidance of Sir Vincent Raven, had been one of the earliest advocates of electric traction and by the time of the Grouping boasted one of the highest route miles of electrified railway among British operators. While the LNER had taken a back seat in the MSJ&A project, they must have been taking notes, for when the government loans of 1935 were made available, the LNER obtained funding for what can only be described as the most adventurous and innovative electrification scheme to date.

The line chosen was a main line that entered Manchester London Road station from the east and originated in Yorkshire at lines from Wath and Sheffield Victoria. These two lines converged at Penistone and then climbed over the Pennines and reached a summit in the 3-mile-long Woodhead tunnel, from where the line descended into Lancashire. Another branch joined the line at Dinting from the market town of Glossop. The route had three main types of traffic. Firstly there was the trunk route express passenger traffic from Sheffield to Manchester, then there were the local passenger trains from Hadfield and Glossop into Manchester, and finally the line had considerable freight traffic in the form of coal from the Yorkshire coalfields for transport across the line and to various points further afield in Lancashire and beyond. The lines had been built by a mix of smaller companies that had merged in 1897 to become the Great Central Railway (GCR). The GCR had become a part of the LNER at the 1923 Grouping. The reasons behind the change to electric traction proposed by the LNER were mainly economical, with the steeply graded nature of the line making it hard work for steam traction. Trains entering the tunnel were burning coal furiously to get their trains to the summit, and one can only imagine what life would have been like for the crews of those machines, enclosed in the tunnel aboard a smoke-bellowing locomotive. Under the LNER proposals, the main-line standard of 1,500 volts DC overhead wires were

A line-up of EM1 locomotives, starting with 26024 and two others, at Rotherwood sidings in Sheffield in 1964. (Basil Hancock)

to be used with a mixture of locomotive-hauled express trains, coal trains and multiple unit local services. The gradient of the line was to be put to another use, with trains climbing uphill requiring current from the overhead lines being offset by trains descending the gradients and braking, their motors acting as generators and thereby feeding current back into the system. This was possible because the physical construction of a DC motor and a DC generator are nearly identical, and by running one in the opposite method you could turn it into the other. The system was known as regenerative braking and had been in use in other parts of Europe for a few years with success. The system would offset some of the costs of buying power in from the national grid and today would be known as 'carbon neutral'. By early 1939 orders were placed by the LNER for seventy locomotives and eight three-car EMUS, with work on the installation of overhead gantries and masts under way, starting from the Manchester end of the line. A total of eleven substations were needed to distribute the power along the entire length of the routes, and work began on constructing and equipping these too. Everything was looking good for the first real main-line electrification north of London when the outbreak of the Second World War put everything on hold. Only projects that were seen as essential for the war effort or those that were close to completion were allowed to continue, as the demand on materials and manpower for the hostilities was far too great and strict priority had to be observed. The Woodhead line was not considered as important or advanced enough, and the works were mothballed for the duration. In 1941 the first locomotive had been completed at the LNER's Doncaster works and was dispatched to the MSJ&A line for trials. It was a box-like structure with a cab at either end and a pantograph above each cab. The wheel arrangement was Bo+Bo, which meant it had two four-wheeled bogies, with a 467 hp traction motor on each axle. Like the MSJ&A motor coaches, these were 750 volts DC motors wired in permanent series. The + meant that the bogies were connected by a pivot and did not swivel independently. The buffers and drawgear were mounted on the ends of the bogie in an arrangement intended to reduce stress on the locomotive's framework. In between the cabs was a compartment containing all the electrical switch gear, traction motor cooling, vacuum brake exhausters and air brake compressors – the loco was fitted with both types of brake, as it was designed for both freight and passenger work. It also featured a steam heating boiler for the latter of the two traffics. The locomotive was finished in LNER green and carried the number 6701. With the conversion of the line it was built to work halted, the locomotive was limited to some basic trial running to identify any shortfalls in the design. There were plenty found, with the ride quality being the biggest issue. The locomotive was prone to rough riding at speeds in excess of 20 mph, and various alternative spring arrangements were tried out to remedy the situation. The locomotive's traction and regenerative braking were put through their paces under the MSJ&A wires; the trials on the latter were difficult to simulate, as the Altrincham route had none of the severe gradients of the Woodhead route. The trial method involved attaching the electric locomotive to one end of a train of wagons and a pair of J39 0-6-0 steam locos at the other, then setting the different forms of traction to work in opposite directions. By October 1941, 6701 had completed trials and the loco was dispatched to her birthplace of Doncaster works for the remainder of the war years. The Woodhead electrification would not be completed for the foreseeable future, and there was no other obvious role for the machine at this time.

By the end of the war it was clear that no decision was going to be made quickly on releasing materials or manpower to resume the work on the project, and the LNER had decided that it would rather concentrate on finishing its Liverpool Street–Shenfield electrification project, which the Ministry of Transport saw as of more national importance in the austere post-war years. No. 6701 was recovered from Doncaster works, renumbered 6000, given a new suspension and shipped to Holland where there was an extensive 1,500 volts DC system that was in need of rebuilding after the ravages of occupation. It arrived there in September 1947. The railway it left behind was about to go through another huge transformation.

As previously mentioned, after six years of wartime control the national network was in a sorry state. Parts of it were unaffected, but where it mattered, in the war-

EM2 Co-Co express passenger locomotive 27000 *Electra* at Sheffield Victoria in 1964. (Basil Hancock)

In the final year of the 1,500-volt DC electrification via Woodhead, 76023 and 76016 running light engine pass Class 506 set 5 at Broadbottom on 9 July 1979. (Basil Hancock)

In their last months, EM1 locos were still doing what they had been built to do without problem. Nos 76010 and 76006 are seen here on a westbound oil tank train at Neepsend, on the outskirts of Sheffield, on 21 July 1980. (Basil Hancock)

torn and bomb-damaged cities, the system was patched up and just about able to keep running. More importantly, the Big Four railway companies were practically bankrupt. The post-war Labour government under Prime Minister Clement Atlee had set out an agenda of state ownership of certain industries, and this included transport, not just rail but road haulage, ports, canals and buses. The means to achieve this was set out in the Transport Act of 1947, which created a central body called the British Transport Commission to administer the running of all of these industries. The running of Britain's railways was handed over to the Railway Executive and they operated under the name British Railways. The shareholders of the former Big Four were compensated from the state purse over a period of years, and it has been argued that the nation paid well over the odds for what was essentially a broken industry. British Railways (BR) came into effect on 1 January 1948. Slowly the branding of the old companies was replaced with the corporate identity of the new; this was gradual at first, with colour schemes being retained for regional components of the 'national' company, often based on the colours of the previous private concern that BR had replaced.

The nationalisation of the railways freed the industry from a number of impasses that had been reached over missing funding to complete various works, the question of the Woodhead route electrification being one such issue. Work was restarted in 1948 to the original plans but the cost soon escalated when it became clear that a new tunnel would need to be bored to replace the two single track ones at Woodhead. To cut back on the escalated costs the proposed

Comparison of front ends of driving trailer M59601M and driving motor M59402M at Manchester Piccadilly on 9 July 1979.

new signalling for the route was cancelled along with the extension of the electrification into Manchester Central and all electric services would now be routed into Manchester London Road. The prototype locomotive was fetched back from Holland in February 1952 and a number of the modifications that had been made to it to improve the suspension and ride were incorporated into the fifty-seven production locomotives that were being rolled out of Gorton works. The production batch featured a few other differences. The train brakes were vacuum only and changes were made to the cab doors. The first nine only were fitted with the carriage heating boiler as the Bo+Bo design was envisaged as primarily a freight locomotive. The first examples were completed in 1950 ahead of the electrification works on the route and went to Ilford for running in trials on the Liverpool Street to Shenfield 1,500 volts DC route. The prototype was renumbered under the BR scheme to 26000 and officially named *Tommy*, which was the affectionate name that had been given to it in Holland and referred to the common name used there to describe a British footsoldier. To handle the express passenger work from Sheffield to Manchester a much larger and more powerful Co-Co locomotive type was built. Seven of these machines were turned out of Gorton Works during 1953/4. They were externally a larger version of the Bo+Bo design with one extra motored axle on each bogie. As they were passenger locomotives steam heat boilers were installed and train braking was vacuum only. The buffers and drawgear were restored to the locomotive body frame in the conventional manner. All seven were painted in

BR black livery and named after characters from Greek mythology. The Bo+Bo locomotives were classified as EM1s and the Co-Co locomotives became known as the EM2s. The original order for eight EMUs for the local services from Manchester to Glossop was not completed until 1954. They bore a similarity to the LMS designs that had appeared on Merseyside fifteen years earlier, and had a driving motor brake third, trailer composite and driving trailer third formation, with the pantograph over the cab end of the driving motor coach. Each axle of that vehicle was fitted with a 185 hp traction motor. The trains had air-operated sliding doors and open saloons but were not provided with gangways between vehicles. As with the LMS Wirral units, the construction was split between Metro Cammell and the BRCW Co.

The electrification was switched on in stages: Wath–Penistone was commissioned in February 1952, but the main line from Sheffield had to wait until the extensive works on the new Woodhead tunnel were completed, and it was

The everyday nature of Manchester–Glossop services is portrayed here, with M59402M at Hadfield on 9 July 1979.

The interior of a Manchester–Glossop unit in BR days, little changed from when built save for the pattern of the moquette. (Basil Hancock)

not until June 1954 that the Manchester–Penistone section went live, followed by Sheffield Victoria–Penistone the following September. By January 1955 the project was completed, heavily over budget but completed nonetheless, and against unbelievable odds. The new electric services shaved considerable time off the previous steam-powered journey times. A Manchester–Sheffield train took only fifty-six minutes under electric power compared to seventy with steam; in the reverse direction the journey time was reduced from sixty-eight to fifty-six minutes. The savings on journey times for freight were even more considerable, with some trains taking half the time they had previously been allocated in steam days. The local service from Manchester London Road to Glossop took ninety minutes, which involved a reversal at Hadfield so both that location and Glossop could be served by one service. Trains departed from Manchester every thirty minutes. Of the eight units built for the route, six were required to be in traffic to fulfil the timetable, something that was never a problem for the type as they proved to be highly reliable. This was to be the first large-scale electrification of a main line in

Britain by 1,500 volts DC, and for reasons of scientific progress it was also to be the last. The nationalisation of the railways had created an environment that was free from inter-industry competition but replaced it with competition from other sources. The Weir committee had identified the rise in private car ownership as a factor that would impact traffic requirements in the future, and that prophecy was proving a reality. Britain's railways now belonged to the nation, but did the nation need them anymore?

Nos 76021 and 76013 on the AC/DC rail tour at Manchester Piccadilly on 16 September 1978. (Basil Hancock)

11

Where Flowers Fade

One railway that had escaped nationalisation was the pioneering Liverpool Overhead. It remained a private concern in charge of its own destiny and finances, free from external controls. The line had opened and business had been good; the extensions had brought in more trade, but the company was never going to be cash rich. The very nature of public transport is that it brings in revenue on a daily basis and that revenue is mostly used up the next day to provide the service, and then the cycle continues. The same is largely true today. The shareholders of the company had received dividend regularly but the LOR held no significant reserves of cash and did not own any major assets; remember it was not built on the ground so had no property of note, except a couple of street-level offices. Its largest single asset was the structure the trains ran on, the steel viaduct that sat 16 feet above the dock road. Its biggest asset also was its biggest liability. The structure was exposed to the elements due to the specific geographical nature of the line, and the damage it had suffered during the war years had also taken its toll. As the LOR began to regroup and move on from the dark days of the Second World War, it revisited its operation and looked at what it would need to do in order to remain competitive in the face of new bus routes, private car ownership and a decline in the use of the docks following the war years. One area it certainly needed to revisit was that of the trains themselves. The fleet was largely approaching fifty years of age in 1948, with the original motor coaches fifty-five years old. There had been many modifications to the traction motors during the intervening years but the basic carriage had remained largely unaltered and looked positively antique. The railway's workshops at Seaforth Sands had carried out a facelift on one driving motor car, No. 29, with a revised cab end. The vehicle emerged in 1945, with new aluminium bodyside panelling but the same door and wooden benches inside. It was followed by a far more comprehensive rebuild to car 30 with tubular-framed seats to replace the original wooden-slatted benches and not only a revised cab as trialled on car 29 but replacement air-operated sliding doors, and the complete body skin was replaced with aluminium panelling and new windows. The original underframe was retained, as were the bogies, albeit after refurbishment of their bearings and springs. The car was finished in a brown and tan livery, a few months after a whole three-car train was modernised to match car 30, formed of cars 30–7–14. The first class car 7 had new hardwood seating with deep, soft upholstered cushions. The train went into service in early 1947 and was joined by a second rebuilt set before the end of the year. Given the limited resources and equipment the team at the LOR workshops had, the standard of the rebuilds was quite impressive and took the trains to a far better level of appearance than would have been thought possible. What the LOR really needed was a fleet of brand-new trains, and they decided to obtain a quote for a new design based upon a three-car formation with steel and aluminium construction. The price they were given was £22,000 per three-car set based upon a minimum order of five complete trains. The LOR would never have been able to afford such an order, so they focused on rebuilding their fleet to the standards already set. Between 1950 and 1955, one complete three-car set was outshopped each year from their workshops.

The LOR had also decided to refocus their advertising on the type of passenger they needed to attract. Their daily commuter traffic was at a regular level but it was between the morning and evening peaks that more patronage was needed, so posters and flyers were produced and distributed with the intention of attracting the sightseeing market, boasting of the unprecedented views of the docks and ships that the line could offer. This was no false claim, as the high walls that surrounded the docks were there to prevent unauthorised access and to keep customs and excise bonded goods safe from unwanted attention. The elevated LOR was simply the only way you could get a good view of the opulent ocean liners moored in the docks following a transatlantic crossing. The campaign did have some positive effects, and sightseeing became another aspect of the LOR's business. Passenger income was stable but never far exceeded operating costs. The General Manager, H. Maxwell Rostron, provided an upbeat assessment of the company's fortunes to the shareholders at their general meeting in 1952, and gave no hint of the dramatic events that were to unfold within the next three years.

As previously mentioned, the unique nature of the line operating for the most part on an iron and steel viaduct just under 6 miles in length was not only a selling point for sightseers, it was also the railway's Achilles heel. The structure had suffered bomb damage in the war, not only from direct hits but also from bombs exploding in the vicinity, which had caused vibration and stress damage. These had all been repaired to keep the railway running, but in haste, and the sections of line that were unaffected by the war had been exposed to sixty years of rain, sleet, snow from above as well as smoke and steam from the steam locos using the dock railway below. The company had a maintenance regime throughout its existence that involved regular inspection and repainting of the plates making up the decking. It is fair to say that maintenance of the LOR could be described as being similar to the job of painting the Forth Bridge – no sooner had it been completed than it was time to start the process again.

A newly modernised LOR unit approaches Seaforth Sands, with the cranes of Gladstone Dock in the background. (Author's Collection)

A rebuilt LOR set rounds the curve into James Street station, with the skyline behind it dominated by the Liver Building, in May 1956. (Jim Peden)

Arguments have been made that the company knew that the structure had a limited lifespan and used this knowledge to reduce its year-on-year maintenance budget in real terms to the point that in the early 1950s it was spending more on the train modernisation project than on repairing the structure. It is not the purpose of this work to put the case one way or the other but to report the facts of what happened next.

The LOR had commissioned a survey of its structure in 1954 and the results, published in a full report in January 1955, made for grim reading. The entire length was in need of renewal, with the decking plates in serious decline in several places due in part to the daily forces that they had to bear from the trains and the environment. The report stated the work would need to be undertaken within the next five years if the structure was to continue to be operated safely. The estimated cost of the work needed was given as just over £2 million. At the time, the LOR earned £150,000 a year in revenue and cost over 80 per cent of that to operate. The idea that such a sum could be found by such a small enterprise, even within five years, was unthinkable. The LOR board recommended that the line be closed, and put the proposal to the shareholders at a General Meeting held in July 1955. The vote was in favour of this option and so the necessary procedures were put in place for the line to be wound down for good. The process involved obtaining parliamentary approval for the closure; this was submitted and received royal assent on 2 August 1956. It gave the final date of operation as Sunday 30 December 1956 and included a proviso that no start could be made to demolish the structure until September 1957, to allow time for an alternative plan to rescue the railway to be made. Once the word got out that the LOR was to close there was considerable outcry and bold attempts were made to save it. Campaigners sought to get the line nationalised as part of British Railways, which would not be accepted as the line was seen by the Ministry of Transport as a local concern and for this reason had been excluded from nationalisation in the 1947 Act. There were also campaigns to get the municipal authority and the MDHB to pump money into the line and keep it open. What prompted this campaigning was that the line was seen as being uniquely Liverpool's, in the same way as the Liver Building was, which was true, as no other city in Britain had a line like the LOR. What went against the campaign to save the line was the political mood toward railways at the time. The 1950s was the decade when the once prosperous and essential metropolitan tramways were being switched off and ripped up across the country on a monthly basis; trams and trains in the cities were seen as old fashioned and out of step with the brave new age of post-war, post-austerity Britain, where every household aspired to own its own car. No amount of sentimental reasoning to save a once ingenious old railway could ever compete with that, just as the trams could not hold back the wave of change. The LOR was doomed and the final day did arrive on 30 December as planned.

A line-up of four LOR units after closure of the line. Pictured in October 1957, they, and the structure they stand on, are waiting for dismantling to begin. (Jim Peden)

A scene of abandonment, with the structure still intact but deserted in October 1957.

In the run-up to final closure there was a surge in patronage, with hundreds wanting to get a final ride on the line; traffic on the final day was especially heavy, with some coming from very far afield to be a part of the passing of this unique line. A bouquet of white chrysanthemums was carried in the cab of the last service to depart from Pier Head south to Dingle, and shortly after the last trains reached their destinations the crowds dispersed, the power was switched off and the LOR passed into history. The structure hung on for just over two years after that night, with the last traces being taken down by January 1959. The carriages were all scrapped save for two examples, and once it was gone the LOR left virtually no trace that it had ever existed. The only physical remains today that are visible are a few of the iron support bases left in a wall near Wapping Dock and the tunnel that carried the line from near Herculaneum Dock to Dingle station. The portal of the tunnel still carries the wording Southern Extension, even if it is a little weather worn since it was opened in 1896; the tunnel has been sealed up, but the Dingle end was used for many years as a car body repair shop. Arguments will continue for evermore over the wisdom in closing the LOR, but post-LOR the very docks it was built to serve would go on to change drastically; one by one they were closed as seaborne freight moved over to a new containerised system, meaning that many of the old docks that the LOR served have been filled in. Today all dock traffic is concentrated on the Port of Liverpool toward the north at Seaforth. Motor car 3, one of the original 1893 vehicles, was saved and is now part of a stunning display at the Liverpool City Museum. The body of modernised first-class trailer 7 also survives, after seeing use as an office in a car scrapyard, and is found at the Electric Railway Museum in Coventry.

A handbill issued in 1949 by the Liverpool Overhead Railway, pitching the line at sightseers rather than the regular traffic of dock workers, in an attempt to increase revenue. (Author's Collection)

12

Colours Fly Away

The formation of British Rail heralded a new era for the electric railways of Liverpool & Manchester, but with it came mixed fortune and a number of changes, to both the visual presentation of the trains and the routes they served. The first change that every passenger, member of staff and casual observer would have seen was the application of a universal colour scheme to all of the various types of multiple units that frequented the networks. The maroon livery of the LMS and the red of the Mersey Railway gave way to British Railways green, and the station name boards changed over time to maroon-backed totems with white lettering, all part of the corporate image of what was now British Railways (London Midland Region). The question of replacing the older pre-Grouping units soon arose, as some of them on the Mersey Railway were approaching their half-century at the dawn of the 1950s. The need to replace the four Wirral line LMS cars lost to wartime bombing was addressed at the same time, when a new fleet of three-car units, identical in nearly every respect, was built by the same manufacturers, and to the pattern of the 1937-built LMS Wirral cars. Only a keen eye could spot the differences; the most obvious one was that on the cars built in 1956 for BR the door open buttons were on the bodyside next to the doors as opposed to on the doors themselves, as was the case with the LMS-built examples. Twenty-four three-car units were built, and in addition two extra driving trailers and two composite trailers were provided to replace those lost in the war; they were re-marshalled with the stored driving motor brakes that made up two hybrid trains of 1938/56 cars. As the new units came out of the builders' works and were commissioned ready for traffic, so week by week rakes of the original Mersey Railway stock were towed away for scrap until just one complete set was left in operation; this clung on until July 1957 when its call to the breaker's yard came, and so the era of the much loved Mersey Railway trains came to an end. One car was earmarked for preservation and was sent to Derby works for storage, but regrettably was destroyed by a fire in the workshop, where it had been placed ready for restoration. The new units were a testament to the reliability and suitability of the original 1937 design, for it has not been known since then for replacement stock to simply be a reissue of a sixteen-year-old design; so suited to the line were these units that in time they themselves became as popular as the faithful old Mersey Railway cars they replaced. The renewal of the stock on the line may well have been a tactic on the part of British Railways, as theirs was no longer the only fixed link between Liverpool and Birkenhead. A road tunnel, known today as the Queensway Tunnel, had opened in July 1934, and, given the rising numbers of privately owned cars, this must have been perceived as a threat to revenue.

Over in Manchester, just before it happened in Liverpool, a pioneering electric line was to close, but the circumstances were very different from those of the eradication of the LOR. The Bury–Holcombe Brook line was withdrawn from the passenger map on 5 May 1952 when passenger services were discontinued. The line had only been added to the electrification of the Bury–Manchester line due to the willingness of Dick, Kerr & Co. to fund their experimental high-voltage scheme along the 3¾-mile route. The L&Y had converted this to match the 1,200 volts DC system of the main route, but now traffic receipts were too low to justify

An LMS-built Wirral set led by M28687M at Birkenhead Central in all-over BR green. (Phil Hughes Collection)

An aerial view of Birkenhead Central in June 1971. The Mersey Railway-built carriage shed was still in use and would continue to be so for many years to come. (Jim Peden)

retaining the branch line electrification and British Railways switched it off, and in time the conductor rails were removed. The line continued to operate for freight trains for several more years and was not closed completely until May 1960; the short section from Bury to Toddington continued to see freight traffic until 1963.

With the withdrawal of the last of the Mersey Railway cars in 1957 the L&Y units that continued to ply their trade between Manchester Victoria and Bury Bolton Street were now almost the only units of pre-Grouping origin left operating on an electrified network in the North West. Trains were being seen as old hat and British Railways was keen to renew the ancient fleet. It had undertaken a programme of stock replacement across the country with a new standard design of carriage being introduced that could be adapted for either locomotive haulage or commuter lines. These became known as the Mark 1 carriage and it was derived from designs previously championed by both the Southern Railway and LMS. All multiple units to be built after 1954 would be based upon this template, with suburban stock having slam doors to every seating bay and semi saloons for third class, as well as compartments with a side corridor; toilets might be fitted to units intended for outer suburban work. The suburban vehicles did not have gangways between coaches, unlike the express versions. When the Manchester–Bury stock

BR-built Manchester–Bury unit, with M65459, leads a train into Bury station on 9 July 1979. (Basil Hancock)

came up for replacement it was to this standard design that the new units were built. Prior to constructing new stock to work on the existing, and unique, 1,200-volt DC system there was an evaluation into changing the electrification for something more standard (shades of the Pringle report). The study proved that simple replacement of the stock was far more cost-effective than replacing the existing conductor rails with either overhead wires or standard conductor rails like the type used on Merseyside. The new units were two-coach sets formed of a driving motor brake and a driving trailer composite; the latter featured both first- and third-class accommodation, with the former vehicle having only third-class accommodation and the space behind the driving cab occupied by the guard's brake. The cabs themselves were more attractive than the flat fronts found on other British Railway suburban Mark 1 units, as the upper area where the cab windows were was angled back, with the flat lower portion housing the multiple working gear and brake pipes for connecting units together when longer trains were needed. Mounted on each axle of the cab-end bogie of the DMB vehicle was a 141 hp English Electric traction motor, with all of the control gear for this in cases between the powered and unpowered bogies. It can be argued that, compared to the futuristic designs that were produced by both the LMS and LNER for their respective electrification works in the 1930s and 1940s, the BR standard units were conservative and functional in design and generally lacked imagination. This was in stark contrast to the strides made in EMU design by the introduction of the L&Y units they were replacing. Twenty-six of these units were delivered during 1959 from BR's Wolverton works, where they were constructed, to Bury Buckley Wells depot. All were finished in the standard BR green livery. The reduced number of vehicles for the new fleet compared to the size of the outgoing L&Y fleet was a reflection on not only the loss of the Holcombe Brook service but the reduction in frequency on the Bury–Manchester line in general. As had been the case with the Mersey Railway cars, the delivery of the new units was followed by a regular procession of the old ones away from the area for scrapping. The last of the L&Y units departed early in 1960 and so the rolling stock legacy of that company came to an end.

This era of rolling stock replacement was against a backdrop of a much larger plan that the British Transport Commission had drawn up for the future of British Railways. Published in December 1954, *The Modernisation and Re-Equipment of British Railways* was an overview of how the BTC saw the industry addressing the issue of bringing the railways into the modern age. The highly ambitious plan, known as 'The 1955 Modernisation Plan', concluded that 'the technical re-equipment of the railways is long overdue', and went on to say that 'despite the growth of alternative forms of transport it is clear that the country must continue to look to the railways to carry the main flows of bulk traffic, both passenger and goods, for many years to come'. The document identified some key objectives that needed to be met in order to give the country 'a railway system which will not only be fully efficient and economic when the Plan is achieved, but will also be adaptable to meet the requirements of many years to come thereafter'. One of these was that steam power should be completely eliminated and no more steam locomotives should be built beyond those already on order. This was not unexpected, as much of Europe and beyond was starting to rid itself of steam power, based upon the availability of coal, the need for better performance and controls of pollutants. The report looked at the alternatives to steam, including a strange paragraph where they concluded that the impact of atomic energy upon the railways was to be indirect and that there would be a ready supply of electricity from atomic power stations, but it was unlikely that an atomic locomotive would ever be built. Electrification was a big part of the plan but one of the factors that held it back from being all dominant was that of cost. The plan stated that electricity had many advantages to the only other alternative, diesel, in that it offered clean operation, reliability and economy in operation with the direct cost per train movement lower than steam, but owing to the high initial cost electrification only becomes financially more attractive where traffic is dense. The plan made clear the BTC's commitment to eradicate steam and replace it with a mixture of both new electrification and diesel-powered trains, all at a cost of £1,200 million. The plan justified this staggering

Bogie and 1,200-volt side-contact shoe gear of M65457 on 9 July 1979. Note the Gresley-style motor bogie. (Basil Hancock)

M65460 undergoing overhaul in Horwich works on 16 August 1980, with a Class 506 car behind. (Basil Hancock)

sum of money by stating that it represented an annual investment of £80 million over its fifteen-year implementation period. All very ambitious indeed but certainly forward-thinking and what the railways needed if they were to stay modern and competitive in the face of fresh competition from the roads in post-war Britain. The only question that needed to be answered was that of which routes were suitable for electrification. The biggest schemes included in the plans were two brand-new main-line projects. One was from King's Cross to Doncaster, Leeds and possibly York; the other was the most significant to our story, as it covered the lines from London Euston to Birmingham, Crewe and onward to Manchester and Liverpool (the West Coast Main Line). However, this was to be a different scheme from the last main-line one that had been carried out between Sheffield and Manchester. The wires of the West Coast Main Line were to carry the new standard of AC current, and to trace the development of that story we must go back in time to the first decade of the twentieth century.

M65457 leads a train into Bury station on 9 July 1979. (Basil Hancock)

13

One Day Like This

The Midland Railway Company were another early entrant to the developing scene of railway electrification. They were not to become prolific in their adoption of it but their one and only venture in the North West would become highly significant in the grand story of how railway electrification developed during the twentieth century. It centred around the county town of Lancashire, Lancaster, which, by 1901, had seen its population almost treble to over 64,000 over forty years. The town was a stopping-off point for the main line from London to Glasgow, and was where the Midland Railway had a branch line that ran via Morecambe to the port of Heysham. The Midland Railway was one of the larger railway companies of the pre-Grouping era, and their empire stretched all the way from London to Derby, Leeds and to the north via the Settle & Carlisle line. The Lancaster–Morecambe line was simply a western extension of their line that had been built to link Leeds with Carlisle. The route started from the London & North Western station at Lancaster Castle then turned off to run into Lancaster Green Ayre station, where a reversal was needed to make the journey over the next section to Morecambe promenade; here, yet another reversal was needed to reach Heysham harbour. Understandably all of the reversing moves in steam days would have required the locomotive to be uncoupled from its carriages and shunted to the other end of the train; to do this twice in one trip meant the journey time was unnecessarily extended. The Midland Railway electrification plans were announced in 1906 and they were different in two respects from any other schemes that had been proposed or constructed by that time. The first was that the conductor chosen to supply current to the trains was to be an overhead wire; while several tramways had adopted trolley wires, which were very similar at this time, no heavy rail operation had done so. The second difference was that the overhead wires would carry a voltage of 6,600 volts AC at a frequency of 25 Hz. The reason for this was simply that the Midland Railway had already installed a generating plant at Heysham Port for running dockside cranes and other equipment, and it was well within the capacity of this unit to supply the railway line too.

The overhead gantries and wires, as installed by the Midland Railway, between Morecambe and Lancaster. (Author's Collection)

AC differs vastly in its properties from direct current. Both rely on the movement of electrons along a conductor, and in both the amount of power it has in that flow is the current and the conductor's ability to inhibit that flow is the resistance. It is the way the current flows that makes them very different. DC will always flow at a constant voltage from the point of source, while alternating current (AC) flows in cycles where the voltage rises from zero to a positive peak and then falls to the opposite negative peak and then back to the zero start point, where the cycle begins again. The number of times this cycle is repeated every second is the frequency of the current flow. When a current is described as having a frequency of 25 Hz it means that the zero–peak–zero cycle is repeated twenty-five times every second. The advantages of AC over DC are many. In a rail application it can be carried over far greater distance from the point of supply and at a much higher voltage, with very little drop in either voltage or current compared to DC, which needs to be topped up at regular intervals by either substations or track paralleling huts or the voltage drop becomes too apparent and the performance of the train will deteriorate as a result. This reduces the installation costs, which were to become a deciding factor in whether a line was economically viable for consideration for electrification. Indeed, while nearly all the electrified lines operating in Britain were supplying their trains with DC, they were all supplied from the national grid by high-voltage AC in the first instance, which then had to be converted to the required DC voltage at a substation. This was because AC had the disadvantage in the early twentieth century that it did not readily lend itself to driving traction motors. The technology existed to produce it and transfer it over long distances to get motion out of it, but the train had to convert the AC into DC on board so the power could be utilised to drive the train along. The equipment needed to do this was a transformer and rectifier, and finding one that was suitable for mounting on a moving vehicle and which could perform reliably in the first quarter of the twentieth century was a gamble, so DC became the supply of choice for Britain's railways save for the two examples already mentioned.

The first of these, the Lancaster–Heysham route, was switched on between Heysham and Morecambe on 13 April 1908, extended to Lancaster Green Ayre on 8 June 1908 and to Lancaster Castle on 14 September 1908. The service used a very unusual collection of rolling stock, all utilising the Sprague multiple unit control system. The vehicles were not like the American-influenced builds seen elsewhere at the time but owed their outline to a more European style. There were two types of carriage. The main ones were the three-bogie driving motor coaches, which were 60 feet long with a cab at each end. Under the floor was the transformer, and this powered the two traction motors. The interior was open saloon and had a sequence of narrow windows down each side, with passenger doors at each end of the vehicle. Seating was transverse at one end and bench seating at the other. The latter was arranged so it gave access to the underfloor equipment. On the roof were mounted two bow collectors, which were held up by compressed air. The vehicle

One of the three double-ended driving motor coaches built for the Midland Railway's Lancaster–Heysham electrification. (Author's Collection)

had a compressor to supply air to these and the train air brakes. To run with these when required were four driving trailers, again with cabs with open saloons. All the seating was on wooden benches and they were not known for their comfort. The electrical equipment was supplied by the German firm Siemens Brothers. The trains could run as either one-, two- or three-coach formations by simply adding driving trailers to the driving motor coaches. The multiple-unit trains sped up the journey time, not just by having superior acceleration to the steam trains but also because they could achieve the two reversals en route in a fraction of the time. The overhead wires were suspended from steel lattice gantries, except at the Lancaster Castle end of the line, where the LNWR had asked for something more attractive to be provided. Here wooden poles were used with a steel span between them from which the conductor wire was suspended.

This first use of AC for rail traction in Britain was joined a year later by a second system established by the London Brighton & South Coast Railway for their commuter lines in South London. This system lasted until 1929, when it was replaced by the third rail, leaving the original Midland Railway scheme (by then part of the LMS) as the sole user. That could have been the end of AC traction if the Pringle report had never been challenged. The standard it set of 1,500 volts DC for overhead wires was the subject of a new study into AC traction supply. Following

A three-car set of Midland Railway-built stock at Lancaster Castle station, with the driving trailer nearest the camera. (Author's Collection)

successful installation of 50-Hz equipment in France, which was inspected by British Transport Commission engineers in 1951, British Railways decided to establish their own test bed for the technology. This involved the conversion of the 25-Hz Midland Railway system to 50 Hz, and the conversion of a fleet of three EMUs to operate the branch. The end for the old Midland Railway units came in February 1951, when the branch was temporarily returned to steam train working while the conversion work was carried out. The main part of the infrastructure was to install a new substation at Lancaster Green Ayre station that took 6,600 volts AC from the national grid and fed it into the overhead catenary. The bulk of the overhead masts from the Midland Railway were reused, with the exception of a ¾-mile section where new-type masts intended for main-line use at higher voltage were erected; some of these were designed to carry wires in limited headroom clearance areas such as under road bridges, and the idea was to evaluate how they worked before making any decision on a wider main-line electrification scheme. The wires themselves for the whole route were replaced with a much thinner grade of cable. The three 'new' units for the line were not new at all but had been withdrawn from traffic in 1940 from the Willesden Junction–Earls Court route, where they had operated since 1914. These three-car units had been built to operate from the fourth-rail DC system and were sent from store to Wolverton works, where engineers from English Electric fitted them out with new motors as well as a pantograph and the transformers and rectifiers they would need to operate from an AC overhead supply. The units were released to traffic for trials from November

1952 and the passenger service went back to electric operation from August 1953. A fourth set was added to the fleet in 1955. Several modifications were carried out over the initial years, with various types of rectifiers, both mercury arc and germanium. Different pantograph styles were also experimented with; the first ones fitted had the traditional diamond shape that was also used on DC overhead systems, or lighter-weight versions of that, but one unit received a French design that had a central single arm to support the collector head.

A report was issued to British Railways late in 1955 by their then Chief Electrical Engineer, S. B. Warder, following a meeting of the International Railway Congress held in London during 1954. In the document the proposals for the new standards for main-line electrification were set out. Warder had studied the use of AC traction supply overseas and gained considerable knowledge from both French and German engineers with experience of AC wires energised at up to 25,000 volts

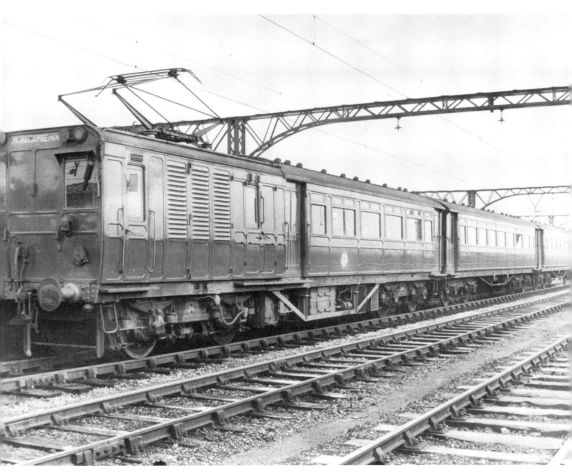

One of the ex-LNWR units after conversion to run on the experimental BR AC electrification that replaced the original Midland Railway scheme. (Author's Collection)

Meols Cop depot, on the West Lancashire Railway section of the original L&Y electrification, was responsible for maintaining not only the LMS-built stock used on the Southport line but the small fleet of units used on the Lancaster–Heysham line during BR days. In this view of 25 October 1964, both types are visible, along with the ex-Tyneside luggage van E68000 that was used at Southport from 1963 to 1967. (Jim Peden)

using a 50-Hz frequency. This, in addition to the experience gained by the use of 50-Hz equipment between Lancaster and Morecambe, convinced Warder that Britain should drop its allegiance to DC for main lines and join the rest of Europe in opting for AC. One hazard he identified was in areas where clearance from the wires to overhead structures, such as bridges and tunnels, was limited. To overcome this he proposed a secondary voltage of 6,600 volts AC be used on the affected section, with the remainder energised at 25,000 volts AC. This went against not only the Pringle and Weir reports but also the recent 1951 study into main-line electrification, which had once again come out in favour of a standard of 1,500 volts DC. The report was accepted and adopted for the main-line electrification work that was to begin in both Liverpool and Manchester.

14

Magic in the Air

No sooner was the ink dry on Warder's report than the massive project to bring AC electrification to the West Coast Main Line began. The 1955 Modernisation Plan was going ahead, and new classes of diesel locomotives were being turned out by manufacturers in small batches for evaluation by BR. The replacement of much of the remaining pre-Grouping rolling stock, both passenger and freight, was in hand, and then there was what was ultimately the jewel in the crown of the plan: the West Coast electrification. Warner had been absolutely right in what he had recommended, and his judgement was based on expert knowledge, sound research and the experience of other similar railways overseas. The high-voltage AC system, while expensive in its initial outlay, would not only speed up the long-distance express trains that ran from Euston to principal cities such as Birmingham, Crewe and on to Liverpool and Manchester, all in direct competition with the proposed M1 motorway, but would also benefit the local services. The decision to leave DC electrification to suburban-only operations made sense, as the long distance involved meant far fewer substations had to be provided; for example only two, 27 miles apart, were needed for the route from Manchester to Crewe. Train performance would be far superior due to the greater amount of current that was flowing in the system.

The work was of course a huge civil engineering undertaking too, with not only the installation of masts and gantries to carry the wires but replacement of signalling, alterations and improvements to stations and construction of new depots and sidings to service the needs of the new electric fleet. To power the express services, a fleet of 100 Bo-Bo locomotives were ordered from five builders. All were to a common specification, required to haul passenger trains at up to 100 mph, and looked very similar to each other, but had differing equipment inside. The details of each type were as follows:

AL1 – These were designed by British Thompson Houston (BTH) and built by the Birmingham Railway Carriage & Wagon Co. of Smethwick. Twenty-five were built and numbered E3001–E3023; a further two were intended to be built with a lower gearing and top speed of 80 mph for freight work, but in the end they

AL1 locomotive, numbered 81016, at Liverpool Lime Street station on 9 September 1974. (Phil Hughes Collection)

AL2, numbered 82003, pictured at Stockport on a southbound parcels train on 16 September 1978. (Basil Hancock)

were completed as per the other twenty-three and the last two were numbered E3096 and E3097. The first of these twenty-five locomotives was delivered on 27 November 1959, by which time BTH had merged with Metropolitan Vickers to become Associated Electrical Industries (AEI).

AL2 – This was a fleet of ten locomotives designed by Metropolitan Vickers and built by Beyer Peacock at their works in Gorton. They were numbered E3046–E3055. There was a flaw in the design stage that would have rendered the locomotives over the specified weight, so a rethink was needed and it was decided to make better use of lightweight aluminium and plastics in these locomotives to make the finished design lighter. The production loco weighed in at 81 tons, only marginally heavier than the AL1. The first example was delivered in 1960.

AL3 – This was a batch of fifteen locomotives designed and built by English Electric at their Newton-le-Willows plant. The first twelve were geared for passenger work and numbered E3024–E3035. A further three were geared for 80 mph freight operation and they were numbered E3303 and E3304, with the final locomotive being numbered E3100, and instead of having 80 mph gearing was delivered with the higher express speed as it was changed to act as a test bed for silicon rectifiers.

AL4 – This was a batch of ten locomotives designed by GEC and built by the North British Company at Springburn in Glasgow. They were numbered E3036–E3045. The first example was delivered in 1960.

AL5 – This was the largest batch and was built in house by BR at their Doncaster works. The fleet totalled forty locomotives numbered E3056–E3095. They were the last to come on stream, with the first example appearing in 1961.

As construction of the various locomotives was commencing, the first section of line to be energised, the routes from Manchester to Crewe, via both Stockport and the Styal loop line, was nearing completion. BR needed something to test on it, having no other AC locomotives it could call upon that could operate at 25 kV. Identifying this need, in 1958 BR authorised the conversion of a redundant experimental gas turbine locomotive that had been built in 1951 for the Western Region to an AC locomotive. The locomotive in question was a Co-Co design, numbered 18100, that had been tested, but the design had not been taken beyond the prototype stage. The machine was taken out of storage and delivered to the Bowesfield works on Teesside, where engineers from Metropolitan Vickers and Beyer Peacock set about converting it. This involved removing the gas turbines and the associated fuel tanks, and installing a transformer and mercury arc rectifiers inside. The loco was also fitted with four traction motors, two less than originally, as the centre axles on each bogie were unpowered, which changed its wheel arrangement to A1A- A1A. The roof at one end had to be altered to accommodate the pantograph, and the cabs were fitted out with controls that matched those to be found in the locomotives then under construction. When finished it was renumbered as E2001. It is important to remember that, while electric traction was by this stage over seventy years old, the change from DC to AC traction was a massive leap in terms of technology. The DC machines were far simpler than the AC variants being introduced, as they featured numerous components and auxiliary equipment, the like of which had never been experienced by either engineers or crews who had spent years working on the DC-equipped routes. The process of staff training was going to be critical for smooth implementation and so it was that E2001 was sent to Manchester for testing and training on the Styal loop line in 1959. In preparation for the electrification, Manchester London Road station was completely rebuilt, and when completed had its name changed to Manchester Piccadilly. In addition to the rebuilding of the station, the nearby locomotive and carriage depot at Longsight was rebuilt and equipped to service the new AC fleets. It got its first taste of things to come when the new four-car EMUs for local services between Crewe and Manchester were delivered. Designated the AM4s, they were of the same basic design as the two-car units being built for the Manchester–Bury DC service. The formation was battery driving trailer, motor brake, trailer composite and driving trailer brake. Each unit had seating for 320 third-class passengers and 19 first. They had a top speed of 75 mph and were fitted with both automatic air and electro-pneumatic brakes. The pantograph was fitted above the guard's brake on the motor coach, which had each of its four axles driven by a 207 hp traction motor. The air compressors were fitted to the battery driving trailer vehicles. All units were painted in the standard BR green livery. They were built at BR's Wolverton works, and deliveries commenced in April 1957 to Longsight, where they had to be put into store until the first stages of electrification were switched on and testing and training could begin. The first batch was for fifteen units, with a second batch of twenty being built for Crewe–Liverpool services.

On 12 September 1960, the service between Manchester Piccadilly and Crewe changed over to AC electrification, with the AM4 units handling the local stopping services and AL locomotives hauling the London-bound trains that now comprised Mark 1 express stock. At Crewe the electric locomotive was detached, and a diesel, or steam, one attached to take the train forward. The reverse applied to Down trains on 12 September 1960 at Crewe. A feature of the new locomotives was their ability to supply electric train heating to carriages, and thus they were not fitted with boilers. A number of the Mark 1 carriages had been built with both electric and steam heating apparatus, so the train was suitably warm regardless of which motive power was on the front.

AL3, by now numbered 83010 and a long way from home at Old Oak Common Open Day on 2 September 1972. (Basil Hancock)

The AL4s, or Class 84s as they became, were rare on passenger work. No. 84010 is pictured on arrival at Glasgow Central on a special on 10 November 1979. (Basil Hancock)

Across to Liverpool, electrification at 25 kV was progressing but it would not be until 1 January 1962 that the section from Liverpool Lime Street to Crewe went live. Again a batch of AM4 units was provided for the local services between the two points, and the depot at Allerton was equipped to service the AC fleet, but the West Coast plan included the provision of a dedicated electric locomotive depot at Crewe. Again, as with the Manchester route, the locomotives were changed at Crewe, and this would be the case until the Crewe–London section of the project could be completed. This would not happen until April 1966, when the first public services between London Euston and Liverpool or Manchester were run without the need for a locomotive change at Crewe. The section of line via Birmingham was added just under a year later, and the southern end of the West Coast was fully electrified. The massive project had not been cheap; each of the 100 new locomotives had cost between £50,000 and £60,000 each, and that was one of the lower costs of the project compared to the thousands of yards of copper wire needed and the man hours it took to install it. The net result was a service that was faster by a considerable margin over longer distances than the one offered in steam days. London–Liverpool could now be done in just under two and three-quarter hours. The local trains benefited from regular departures at the same minutes past each hour, and to all living and working on the route the future of railways had arrived with the realisation of the Modernisation Plan. But the politicians had other ideas.

BR-built AL5, numbered 85037, pictured towing a very mixed rake on a parcels train at Lancaster on 20 August 1980. (Basil Hancock)

Class 115 DMU and AM4 unit 304027 at Liverpool Lime Street station in April 1976. (Phil Hughes Collection)

No. 304042 at Manchester Oxford Road on 20 July 1987. (Basil Hancock)

No. 304001 at Sandbach on 20 March 1976. (Basil Hancock)

English Electric-built locomotive AL3, by now classified as Class 83 and numbered 83 003, is seen here stabled at Liverpool Lime Street between duties in 1974. (Phil Hughes Collection)

15

This Charming Man

The British Transport Commission were so confident in the wording of their 1955 Modernisation Plan about railways and how they had a future that they stated, 'The train mileage predicted for 1970 will not be very different in total, being estimated at 204 million.' They had utter belief that £1,200 million spent on the plan would deliver the railway Britain both needed and deserved. The biggest problem with this was that the BTC were spending money they didn't have. The Government of the age was led by Prime Minister Harold MacMillan, who had been re-elected in 1959. MacMillan appointed a new Transport Minister for this second term, Ernest Marples. Marples had previously been the Postmaster General, and during his term in that office had overseen the introduction of both the premium bond and postcode schemes. He also had business interests in the construction industry through the firm Marples Ridgway, which he had co-founded in 1948. As Minister for Transport, one of his briefs was to stem the haemorrhage of money passing from the Treasury to the railways, which were estimated to be making losses in the region of £300,000 per day. An advisory group to report on the state of British transport, not just rail, was established in 1960 under the chairmanship of Ivan Stedeford. Stedeford had approached Sir Frank Smith, a former engineer from ICI, to sit on the committee, but Smith declined the invitation. However, he offered another name that might be suitable: Dr Richard Beeching. Beeching was a current member of the ICI board. He accepted the offer and joined the Stedeford committee, where he subsequently clashed with the chairman on a number of issues. The committee's report has never been made public but what happened after its publication is very well known. In March 1961 Beeching was appointed as Chairman of the British Transport Commission. He was in effect appointed by Marples to oversee its demise. The passing of the Transport Act in 1962 both dissolved the BTC and passed its responsibility for railways to the British Railways Board (BRB) with effect from 1 January 1963. The first Chairman of the BRB was Richard Beeching. Another clause of the 1962 Act was that the formal closure process for railway lines was made simpler.

The cover of the infamous *The Reshaping of British Railways* report, better known as The Beeching Report. (Crown Copyright)

By 1963 branch line closures were not a new thing by any means. The Branch Line Committee set up by the BTC in 1949 had closed over 3,000 miles of railway lines that were little used and very uneconomic, one example being the Holcombe Brook line mentioned earlier. This was to be a precursor, for Beeching had the belief that the railways must be made more profitable and not dependent on government subsidy. The brief that had been handed down to him made clear that the railways needed to be 'reshaped to meet the modern requirements and their prospects, and the modernisation plan should be adapted to this new shape'. The BRB under Beeching was to present a report on how to achieve this, entitled *The Reshaping of British Railways*, and its publication on 27 March 1963 created shock waves that were felt across Britain. Beeching's report focussed on lines that could not be run at a profit and also on routes that were directly competing against each other. While it was very true that rail traffic had declined over the previous decades with the rise of car ownership and the end of petrol rationing, it was also felt that with the railways under state ownership their duty was to provide a public service, even an unprofitable one. Beeching disagreed, and his report recommended the closure of 5,000 miles of track and 2,363 stations. It also proposed an end to handling wagon load freight traffic and a move to modal containerised freight. The report did identify areas where investment would bring about benefit to the railways, one such area being the extension of West Coast electrification from Crewe to Glasgow. The public was not interested in the proposed investments; what caught their attention were the widespread closures that were being proposed. It is not the intention of this book to evaluate the rights and wrongs of the Beeching report in general but to look at how the proposals affected the electric railways of the North West. The lines had been electrified in the first place to make them more competitive and increase their revenue. The investment made by those earlier generations was now going to be tested to the maximum. If a line could not be operated at profit then it was threatened, so how did the electrified network hold up against those lines that were operated by diesel or the dwindling number of steam engines?

If you obtain a copy of *The Reshaping of British Railways* and turn to page 102, there, in geographical order, is the list of complete routes that were to be closed. There were five and a half pages of them. Page 104 contained five routes familiar to our story:

Manchester Victoria–Bury Bolton Street
Southport Chapel Street–Crossens
Liverpool Exchange–Southport Chapel Street
Lancaster Castle–Lancaster Green Ayre–Heysham
Manchester Piccadilly–Hadfield/Glossop

While the Southport–Crossens service may have been expected, the others were a complete shock to local residents. Although the main Woodhead route from

With the end in sight for the class and their route, farewell specials were run using the EM1s. Here 76021 and 76013 are on the AC/DC rail tour at Manchester Piccadilly on 16 September 1978. (Basil Hancock)

Sheffield to Manchester Piccadilly was not threatened, the local service from Manchester to Hadfield and Glossop was to be withdrawn. Beeching also proposed the complete closure of the non-electrified alternative route between Sheffield and Manchester via the Hope Valley. The proposal to close the Manchester–Bury Bolton Street service would leave Bury without a rail service. Both Bury and Southport were being selected as locations where, despite there being no competing rail routes and the line not making substantial losses, it was considered that bus services could replace the trains and be run far more cheaply. You do have to wonder if the author of the report had ever ventured on to the roads in these areas. One other line on the list was the ex-Midland Railway route from Lancaster to Heysham. This was a line that had competition from another rail route, but it was the electrified one of the two that was threatened with closure. The Beeching report was met with waves of protest, but the BRB and the government accepted it. However, in October 1964 the British people rejected MacMillan's government in favour of a Labour one under Harold Wilson. Wilson appointed Barbara Castle as Minister for Transport, and their promise to re-evaluate the closure programme was a double-edged sword. In June 1965 Richard Beeching left his post at the BRB to return to ICI. By the end of 1965 some 2,000 miles of line had been closed, which included the electric service from Southport to Crossens that had seen its last train on 5 September 1964. On 3 January 1966 the Lancaster–Morecambe portion of the Midland Railway route was closed and so ended the link to the first AC overhead line. The portion from Morecambe to Heysham was retained, but only a limited service operated to connect with sailings from the port at Heysham. In time all the electrification equipment was removed as the line was now diesel operated.

This left the Liverpool Exchange–Southport, Manchester Victoria–Bury, and Manchester Piccadilly–Glossop services still under threat. Events were to transpire to reprieve all three, but at a cost. The reasoning behind some of the proposed closures was the number of competing routes. Sheffield–Manchester had two such links: the electrified Woodhead route and the non-electrified route via the Hope Valley. While this was competition if you were travelling from one city to the other, that's where the competition ended, as for all the intermediate stations on the route that was your

With the locos being disposed of, they were cannibalised for their bogies to keep the final ones in service. This photograph was taken at Reddish depot on 27 July 1981, with withdrawn Class 76 loco bodies and Class 506 set 7. (Basil Hancock)

only choice of rail service to either of those cities. In a surprise move the axe was lifted from the Hope Valley line, and the Woodhead route was threatened with closure. The Glossop service was reprieved but the through passenger services from Sheffield were axed. The EM2 Co-Co locomotives that were built exclusively to work the line were taken out of traffic in September 1968. The remaining months of passenger traffic were left to the Class EM1 locos, a few of which had been built with train heating boilers for this purpose. On 5 January 1970 the passenger trains ran for the last time, and the route became a freight-only line for just over another decade. It closed in July 1981 and all but one of the EM1s went for scrap; the sole survivor is now preserved at the National Railway Museum in York. The EM2s were stored for a period in the car shed at Bury. As they were only fifteen years old, the whole class was nowhere near life expired. The Dutch national railway operator, Nederlandse Spoorwegen (NS), inspected them and bought all seven for use on their 1,500-volt DC network, where they were employed until 1986. The locos were exported, and six of them underwent modifications to make them suitable for traffic in Holland; the seventh was cannibalised for spares. Upon retirement two of the class were repatriated for preservation. No. 27000 *Electra* is at the Midland Railway Centre with 27001 *Adriane*, gifted to the Manchester Museum of Science & Industry on condition it remains in NS livery. A third locomotive, 27003 *Diana*, is preserved in Holland.

The only surviving EM1, 26020 (76 020), is part of the national collection, and is pictured here on display in the Great Hall in 1987. (Graeme Gleaves)

As the 1960s drew to a close, the railways began to regroup after the most traumatic decade of their existence. It was perhaps a testament to their original proposers that most of the network survived and was ready to face the next chapter in the story of our railways when so many other lines did not. The railways had to face up to the facts that their golden age was long gone and they had to justify their continued existence. The Beeching era had also served as a warning, to those who cared, that if railways were to continue to be a part of the fabric of society, then society would need to play a part in supporting them.

Repatriated from Holland and restored in Britain, EM2 27000 *Electra* is on display in 2014 at the Midland Railway Centre at Butterley. (Graeme Gleaves)

16

Whole Again

The 1970s was to be a decade of significant changes to the long-standing suburban electrified lines around both Liverpool and Manchester. In the case of the latter, the biggest project was the conversion of the original MSJ&A 1,500-volt DC overhead electrification to 25 kV AC to match the West Coast Main Line. The service from Altrincham was cut back to go only as far as Manchester Oxford Road from 1960 when Piccadilly station was rebuilt. By 1970 the original MSJ&A trains were thirty-nine years old and in need of replacement, as was much of the overhead equipment. British Railways decided that to best integrate the line with its other electric services in the area, it would be converted to 25 kV AC overhead, and AM4 units were brought in to work the line. The work was completed in May 1971 and thus 30 April was the last day of 1,500 volts DC on the route to Altrincham, with the AC EMUs taking over from 3 May. The Manchester–Hadfield and Glossop service continued to operate as the last outpost of 1,500 volts DC for now. Another change that occurred was a mass re-livery of the trains. The green of the 1950s gave way to all-over blue towards the end of the 1960s on the suburban stock, while the loco-hauled fleet on the West Coast gained a blue and grey livery, with the grey area being the upper half of the body. New coaches classified as the Mark 2 had begun to appear, and these had stronger bodies and improved heating and lighting. An air-conditioned variant was produced and this was used as the stock for both the Manchester and Liverpool Pullman services introduced in 1966. The accommodation was first class only on the Manchester one, and both services offered the best journey time in each direction between their relevant city and London. The livery was a reversal of the normal BR blue and grey, with the light grey being on the lower bodyside. The coaches were purpose built and had features not found on other Mark 2 carriages, such as inward-opening passenger doors. The Liverpool train was not as popular as the Manchester one, and was taken off the timetable in the mid-1970s; the Manchester one lasted until 1985. New locomotives also appeared on the West Coast from August 1965. The AL6 was a Bo-Bo like the first batches of AC loco, and 100 were built. The higher-speed services were marketed under the Inter-City branding from 1966, the hyphen being dropped from the name within a couple of years.

No. 81008 takes the Manchester Pullman set north past the Leyland Trucks factory at Leyland on a special on 5 September 1981. (Basil Hancock)

M28587M leads a train at Manchester Oxford Road on 13 January 1971. Despite the old BR green livery, it has the modern single arm pantograph. (Basil Hancock)

The way British Rail referred to its trains changed in 1968, when it adopted a computer-based system, called TOPS, to keep track of them. Every locomotive, carriage, wagon and multiple unit had to be recorded in the system, so locomotives and multiple units were classified by TOPS codes. The ones that affect our story were as follows:

AC locomotives AL1–AL6 became TOPS classes 81–86 respectively.
DC Locomotives EM1 and EM2 became TOPS classes 76 and 77 respectively.
AM4 units became TOPS class 304.
LMS Southport units became TOPS class 502; Wirral units became TOPS class 503.
BR Manchester–Bury units became TOPS class 504.
Original MSJ&A units became TOPS class 505; Glossop units became TOPS class 506.

The 1970s saw massive changes to the electrified railways on Merseyside. The lines comprised two parts: there were the routes of the former Mersey and Wirral railways, and on the Liverpool side of the river were those of the former Lancashire & Yorkshire Railway, which ran from Liverpool Exchange north to Southport and Ormskirk. The two networks were both electrified by third rail, but had no physical connection between them and offered no real advantage to each other in terms of service connections. As far back as the early 1960s it had been proposed that the suburban network should be remodelled to make it more integrated with the needs of the city. The first steps toward this were taken in 1968, with the creation of the Merseyside Passenger Transport Authority (MPTA) to manage not only trains but buses and ferries serving the Merseyside area. The MPTA was a proactive organisation in overseeing a plan to rebuild the railways under Liverpool.

Work on the scheme commenced in 1972 and the plan was for the existing Mersey Railway line to become a circular loop under the city. Trains running from the Wirral would travel round the 3.2 km loop in a clockwise direction, serving new stations at Moorfields, Lime Street, a new deep-level station at Liverpool Central and then back under the river after leaving James Street station. The junction on the Birkenhead side of the river was rebuilt to allow for an increased number of services to run from Rock Ferry and the lines from Birkenhead North. In 1973 work commenced on the reconstruction of the lines on the Liverpool side of the river. The plans, when completed, saw the closure of Liverpool Exchange station and the construction of a new tunnel to take the line under the city and south to link up to Garston. The 'new' line used part of the original Mersey Railway line, including the original Liverpool Central station. There was also a service tunnel between the link and loop lines to allow for the exchange of stock between the Wirral and Southport lines for the first time. An addition to the electrified network

Class 502 unit, M29890M, in all-over BR blue at Garston on 5 May 1979. (Basil Hancock)

on the Liverpool side was the electrification of the short branch from Sandhills to Kirkby; this was to present a new area of operation for the 503 units, as four of them were drafted in from the Wirral to provide stock for the service from Garston to Kirkby when it commenced in 1977. Because the new loop line the 503s were going to work in was a single tunnel, the whole fleet had to be rebuilt to comply with safety regulations before the loop was opened in 1977. The work was undertaken at Horwich from 1972. It involved fitting doors, with handrails, in the ends of each vehicle, including the cab ends, to allow a train to be evacuated in a single-bore tunnel. At the cab ends, the pair of air pipe connections had to be duplicated, one pair either side of the door. There were also modifications to the current collection equipment, which originally was mounted on the leading bogies of the driving cars and was now confined to the bogies of the driving motor coach only. The Link line had none of those problems, and the 502 units needed no modifications. The whole fleet of both classes were repainted into the same blue and grey colour scheme as the InterCity coaches from the mid-1970s.

The construction of the Loop and Link lines in Liverpool had breathed new life into the transport network, but it had showed the age of the existing units, and as

Comparison of Wirral Class 503 sets at West Kirkby on 5 May 1979 after modifications for Loop line working. (Basil Hancock)

Class 503s M28394M (built 1956) and M28690M (built 1938) at Southport on the farewell tour for the class on 13 April 1985.

the 1980s began plans were under way for the replacement of the LMS designs. New suburban units had started to be delivered to British Rail from 1976, built to modern standards, with sliding doors, electric brakes and saloon interiors lit by fluorescence. In many ways the new stock was to bring the same benefits that had come with the introduction of the 503s themselves. The design was a new BR standard for inner suburban routes, and could be built for either third rail or overhead AC. It had been tested with three prototype units, two four- and one two-car units, designated the PEPs. These were tested in both Scotland and the south of England before production classes began to appear. The first to arrive were thirty-three units classified Class 507, formed with two driving motor coaches and an intermediate trailer. None of the units derived from the PEP design had toilets, and all had 3+2 low-backed seating. Tied in with the Loop line project was the construction of a new depot at Kirkdale to maintain the fleet on the Liverpool side; this followed the demise of Meols Cop shed, which had closed in 1970. The units built to replace the 503s (known as Class 508 units) started to be delivered in 1979, but the 503s were not immediately withdrawn, as a change of policy meant their replacements were sent to work in south-west London and Surrey, where

No. 508 137 at Southport station in 1996. (Graeme Gleaves)

Merseyrail-liveried 507 028 at Kirkdale depot in 1997. (Graeme Gleaves)

it was considered they were more urgently needed. This reprieve proved only temporary, and the 508 units started to be delivered to Merseyside from 1982; the last 503s were taken out of service on 29 March 1985. A farewell trip in the whole electrified Merseyrail network, both Wirral and Southport lines, was run on 13 April 1985 using a unit of 1938 and one of 1956 vintage. The 508s were nearly identical to the 507s but had been built as four-car units. One of the intermediate trailers was removed from the formation prior to delivery to Merseyside, and was retained by the Southern Region for inclusion in a future build of units. These two classes still provide all third-rail services on Merseyrail at the time of writing. A single example of each of the 502s and 503s has survived into preservation.

17

I Am the Resurrection

Having experienced the lows of the 1960s and regrouped in the 1970s, the 1980s could have offered a mixed bag of fortunes for both the Merseyside and Manchester networks. The railways in general were not held in high public regard, with complaints about punctuality, cleanliness, staff helpfulness and price being constantly voiced in both local and national media. The creation of local Passenger Transport Executives had devolved some influence on how railways were run and how money could be found and spent on improvements from Westminster and into the hands of local politicians. The Merseyside PTE had been instrumental in the creation of the Loop and Link lines during the 1970s, and across Lancashire in Manchester the creation of its PTE happened in stages. The first immediately followed the 1968 Transport Act that authorised the setting up of such bodies with the formation of the South East Lancashire North East Cheshire Passenger Transport Executive (SELNEC) in 1969. The new body wasted no time identifying one of its major projects: the poor links between the two main stations in the city, Piccadilly and Victoria. Like London, none of the major stations were in the city centre; they had been built on what were then the outskirts. London had solved this problem and linked up its many termini with the creation of the Underground network; Manchester had the issue on a smaller scale, and it was never considered to take action to link the two railway hubs with another railway until SELNEC proposed just such a scheme. The proposal for a Picc-Vic underground railway was presented in 1971 and comprised a tunnel linking the two stations running under the city, with three intermediate stations, linking into the national network at either end. The proposal had merits and was approved of by local business and residential users, but it did not get much further than the drawing board and was abandoned in 1977. At the time SELNEC was being replaced by a new PTE that reflected Manchester's status as a Metropolitan Borough; the new body, called the Greater Manchester Passenger Transport Executive (GMPTE), took over the role of SELNEC in 1974. Despite the cancellation of the Picc-Vic tunnel, the GMPTE would continue to look at the issue of improving rail links across the city.

Class 504 M65461 leads a set in GMPTE livery at Manchester Victoria on 20 July 1987. (Basil Hancock)

British Rail had decided to rid itself of the last vestiges of the old 1,500-volt DC overhead system and set about the conversion of the Piccadilly–Hadfield and Glossop line to 25 kV AC overhead to make it standard with the other lines in the area. The work was a repeat of that carried out on the MSJ&A just over a decade earlier. The 506 units operating the line were the last 1,500-volt DC units operating in Britain, and were thus non-standard. They were withdrawn after a final day of service on 7 December 1984, and after that AC EMUs operated the service. At first these were Class 303 units displaced from the Glasgow suburban network, but in time they were returned to their former haunts, and the line came to be worked by Class 304s and their near identical cousins, the 305 units, which had been displaced from Liverpool Street suburban services. So the last remnants of the LNER, both in terms of rolling stock and the legacy of its electrification, disappeared from the national network.

While British Rail had carried out the conversion work, the GMPTE had been busy drawing up proposals of its own to rejuvenate suburban travel in and around Manchester. In 1982 they stated that a light railway system was their preferred option to link the city centre, both termini, and the routes that fanned out from them. The GMPTE felt the electrified heavy rail routes were mostly underutilised and not offering the best they could to travellers. This was certainly true of the Bury route, where the service had been cut back drastically to the point that half of

One of the 100-strong batch of Class 86 (AL6) locomotives stands at the head of an Up Liverpool express, having just arrived at Euston. (Graeme Gleaves)

the fleet of 504 units was now in store. The line did, however, manage to operate with very high levels of punctuality, mainly due to its self-contained nature. The GMPTE set up a rail study group to examine the options to support its proposed light rail scheme, and representatives from local councils and British Rail joined this. The group delivered their proposals in 1984, which were as follows. There would be three routes. The first was a link up of the former MSJ&A route from Altrincham to a city centre tramway that would pass under Manchester Piccadilly and then link up with the Hadfield and Glossop line; both the heavy rail routes would cease to be operated by BR. The second route was a diversion of the Bury–Manchester Victoria route to join the city centre tramway and then link up to a section of the Hope Valley line to Rose Hill and Marple. The third route was to connect the Oldham line to Manchester city centre. All services would be run at ten-minute intervals by two-car units powered from overhead wires electrified at 750 volts DC. The trains were referred to as 'Super Trams', which was very apt for they took the best features of the tram and fused it with the best features of the electric multiple unit. Politics again intervened in the smooth running of the GMPTE when the Local Government Act was passed in 1985 and abolished the metropolitan councils, including the Greater Manchester County Council, and the GMPTE was thereafter made up of representatives from the ten district councils that had replaced the metropolitan authority.

Class 305 unit 305 506 arrives at Manchester Piccadilly from Glossop. The unit wears a variation of Regional Railways livery. (Graeme Gleaves)

The Metrolink proposals were further enhanced in 1987, with additional proposals added to the scheme in the shape of additional lines to both Rochdale and Salford Quays. The biggest statement of intent for the project was the establishment of a short demonstration line in March 1987 at Debdale Park, where nearly a mile of track of a disused goods line was electrified with overhead wires, and a two-car Docklands Light Rail unit, borrowed from that operator ahead of its opening, was run to demonstrate the benefits of the new generation of Light Rapid Transit (LRT) units from a temporary platform. The formal proposals to create the network were submitted to Parliament, and the brand name of Metrolink was unveiled at a press conference. The Greater Manchester (Light Rapid Transit System) Act 1988 was passed in January 1988, and the project had the go-ahead. A consortium was formed by the successful bidders for the construction and conversion of the infrastructure, namely the GMPTE, AMEC Plc, John Mowlem Plc and GEC Transportation Projects Ltd, all under the name of Greater Manchester Metrolink Limited (GMML).

Construction work began in 1990 and started in the city centre, where the streets had to be dug up so railway lines could be installed with their top surfaces flush with the street level. The overhead catenary was of a lighter type than that used for BR-type AC electrifications, and platforms in the city had to be built to match the height of those on the former BR lines over which the Super Trams were to run. In order to change the first lines over to tram operation, their BR services had to be closed and replaced by buses. The first two routes selected for phase one of the Metrolink were the Manchester Piccadilly–Altrincham and Manchester Victoria–Bury ones. The Glossop route had been shelved from the plan. The Bury line was closed entirely by August 1991, and the remaining fleet of Class 504 units went for scrap, except for two, one of which still survives at Bury in the care of the East Lancs Railway Preservation Society; the other was with them too for a while, but was broken up for spares. The MSJ&A closed on 24 December 1991, and the 304s went on to other work in the North West and Midlands before they were all withdrawn and sent for scrap in 1996; none of the type survived into preservation.

The conversion work of the former BR lines retained the original track alignments and stations, but new signalling and overhead catenary to match that of the street sections had to be installed, a few new stations were added and others had their names changed. The first public service ran on 6 April 1992 between Bury and Manchester Victoria. The next phase to be opened was from Victoria to the G-Mex three weeks later. The Altrincham line became operational on 15 June, with the final section into the underground terminus at Manchester Piccadilly opening on 20 July, three days after Queen Elizabeth II had performed the official opening ceremony for the system.

Liverpool had linked all of its city centre railways in the 1970s with the creation of the Loop and Link lines; the 1980s and 1990s were to see further extension.

No. 303049 at Glossop in GMPTE livery on 24 October 1986. (Basil Hancock)

The Loop and Link were completed after nearly six years' construction. The lines to Southport and Ormskirk via the Link were called the Northern Lines and the former Mersey Railway route from Liverpool and on to the Wirral Peninsula became known as the Wirral Lines. All routes were by now electrified by the third rail at the standard 750 volts DC. At the same time, the line from Kirkdale to Kirkby was also electrified. The Link line electrification was extended further south to Hunts Cross in 1983.

Over on the Wirral Lines, the third rail was extended much further. The section from Rock Ferry to Hooton was energised from 30 September 1985, with the last surviving LMS-built Class 503 unit forming a ceremonial opening train. From there it went further south on 3 September 1993 to Chester. The branch from Hooton to Ellesmere Port joined the electrified network on 29 May 1994. In 2011 the Mersey electric network was responsible for over 100,000 passenger journeys per day, serving sixty-seven stations. The system is recognised as one of the most reliable operators in terms of train performance, with levels of punctuality recorded that have consistently put it at the top of Department for Transport league tables. Further expansion of the electrified network is being considered.

Above ground, the AC electrification has seen new services and stock to work them. The creation of a station at Manchester airport resulted in Class 309 units

No. 304043 at Altrincham on 9 July 1979. (Basil Hancock)

being brought in from Essex after they were displaced from their former haunts. The run up to privatisation saw many new liveries appear, with GMPTE sponsored services appearing in two tone brown, with blue and grey giving way to the dark grey, red, white and beige on the InterCity fleet. Some other services appeared in Regional Railways livery, including the 309s, which was mainly a rich blue with light grey and a green stripe.

The privatisation of the former British Rail network took place in stages from 1996 onwards with the stations, track and signalling becoming the property of Railtrack and the train services being operated under franchise by a number of private operators. The franchises are divided on a regional route basis and have changed hands several times. The companies that bid for them are a mix of bus operators and other transport companies from overseas who enter into partnership with UK concerns. Railtrack proved to be a disaster for the government and they took the extreme step of taking it over and placing the infrastructure, and its maintenance, back into public ownership under the name of Network Rail (NR). NR is run not for profit and reinvests its operating surplus into improving the network. It also gets funding from the Treasury over five-year periods which it must outline prior to applying for the funds from the public purse. Each five year plan, called a control period, contains details of what projects are to be started and completed during the five year life cycle of the control period. The government then decides how much funding will actually be authorised. As can be expected in an arrangement of this sorts the difference between what NR asks for and what it gets is often considerable.

One project that was started by Railtrack and completed by Network Rail was the complete upgrade of the West Coast Main Line. Under the plan the track was upgraded to enable trains to run at speeds of up to 140 mph for stretches. These would not be the old loco-hauled trains as they were going to be phased out and replaced by a fleet of streamlined units built especially for the route. The Pendolinos (Class 390) are based on an Italian design and feature a tilting body system that smoothes out the centrifugal force as a train negotiates a curve at speed. The units were built as nine-car sets (some subsequently lengthened to eleven cars) with all vehicles passenger carrying. Traction packages are of the three phase type which use AC motors and high performance electric brakes are fitted. The trains are fully air conditioned. The first batch were constructed by Alsthom at the Washwood Heath plant that was formerly Metro Cammell, Alstom having bought them out in the 1980s. When Alstom closed that plant in 2005 construction of the remaining vehicles was switched to Italy. The West Coast Main Line upgrade ran horrifically late and over budget. It was not completed until December 2008 and certain aspects of the project had to be cancelled to save costs. One part of the project not to be included in the final roll out was the in cab signalling that would enable the Pendolinos to run at 140 mph. Instead the top speed was capped at 125 mph, which still enabled significant chunks to be knocked off the point-

'Supertram' set 1026 at Piccadilly Gardens with a service for Eccles in 2013. (Graeme Gleaves)

to-point timings of the route. London–Manchester was now two hours and six minutes. The first Pendolinos ran in July 2002 on the Euston–Manchester route and were a welcome addition to the service as the city was hosting the Commonwealth Games at the time.

The Metrolink has expanded several times since phase one was opened. In 1997 construction of a route to Eccles began with the first section as far as Broadway opening in December 1999 and the remainder of the branch carrying its first passengers in July 2000. The Princess Royal performed an official opening ceremony for the line in January 2001. Metrolink operations were taken over under a franchise agreement by the Stagecoach Group in July 2007; they set up a subsidiary company, Stagecoach Metrolink, to manage this contract. The operator does not own the track or trains, and simply provides the service in much the same way as the franchise holders do on the former BR network. The latest extension to the network is the Oldham and Rochdale line. In the summer of 2014 the fleet of original Super Trams was withdrawn and replaced by new-builds; one unit was saved and is due to be presented to the Heaton Park Tramway Museum.

In July 2012, as part of Control Period Five, Network Rail obtained funding for several new 25-kV electrification schemes. One of these will see the route between

Second-generation 'Supertram' unit 3027 at Piccadilly Gardens, bound for Metrolink Manchester Piccadilly terminus. (Graeme Gleaves)

Hunslet-built Class 323 three-car EMU at Manchester Piccadilly in June 2013. These units feature three-phase drive, and arrived in the area following displacement from their original routes in the Midlands. (Graeme Gleaves)

Liverpool Lime Street and Manchester Piccadilly electrified – the first time these two cities have been linked by electrification. Given that they, and the north-west region around them, have acted as the cradle for nearly all railway electrification that has happened to date in the UK, it is a fitting tribute to those visionaries who first thought that electricity really was the future for rail that these railways have not only survived and endured but have gone on to flourish and expand. It is certain that if this book is rewritten in another twenty years there will be plenty of new material to report on; that is what the story of the electric railways in the North West has always been about: progress.

Virgin Pendolino unit 390 151 stands at London Euston on 23 November 2014, forming the 20.05 service to Liverpool Lime Street. These units offer a level of service that was unimaginable when the first electric trains ran in Liverpool 121 years earlier. (Graeme Gleaves)

Appendix 1

Electric Locomotives of the Lancashire & Yorkshire Railway

The bulk of the services operated in this story have been of the multiple-unit type. The only exceptions are the Woodhead and West Coast Main Line express trains and the goods trains on the former. The suburban nature of the early operations did not lend itself to locomotive haulage, and thus electric locomotives were not produced for either the Liverpool Overhead or Mersey Railway. The Lancashire & Yorkshire Railway did experiment with electric locomotives from an early time and in a limited number – just two. Their story makes an interesting add-on to the main tale of the electric railways.

The Aintree Beetle

Locomotive No. 1 was built at Horwich works in 1912. The engineer responsible for this contraption was George Hughes. His design used the chassis of a 2-4-2 tank engine, upon which was constructed a body, with a central cab and lower bonnet ends. Mounted each side in front of each pony truck was a collector shoe for the live rails. On one end of the central cab was a spring-loaded bow collector that was used in the yard at Aintree sorting sidings, where the provision of conductor rails was impractical and thus overhead wires were erected. Inside the locomotive were four 150 hp motors, which in turn were connected to jack shafts that drove the coupling rods on the four driving wheels. The motors were supplied by Dick, Kerr & Co., the supplier of choice for all the L&Y electric stock.

In practice this locomotive was highly unsuccessful. It was intended for freight shunting and working wagon loads over short distances, but rarely ventured outside Aintree yard. Reports from those who did work with it described it as a poor and rough runner, and its design meant that every jolt from a joint in the track was amplified. The loco was withdrawn around 1919, and is believed to have been scrapped by 1922.

Locomotive Number 2

A much smaller, but more successful, loco was built for the L&Y to shunt coal wagons at Clifton power station on the Manchester–Bury line. It was a four-wheeled affair with a central steeple cab, and was built around 1918. The bonnets contained batteries that powered the two 18 hp motors, and it could run for 25,000 miles between charges. It too was built at Horwich works, and remained at Clifton until LMS days in 1946, whereupon it was reportedly transferred to Greenhill sleeper works in Derby before being scrapped around 1947.

Appendix 2

Notes on Chapter Titles

Most people will not think of electric railways when you mention the names of Liverpool and Manchester to them. Most will think of two things in popular culture for which the region is famous: the sporting rivalry of its football teams, and the hundreds of bands that have come from the region and been responsible for millions of record sales. The North West can lay claim to a disproportionate number of successful and influential acts, and in honour of that each chapter of this book has the song title from a band associated with Liverpool, Manchester or the surrounding area. The full list is as follows:

Chapter 1 – 'A Northern Soul' by The Verve, a track from their 1995 album 'A Northern Soul'.

Chapter 2 – 'The Long & Winding Road' by The Beatles, a track from their 1970 album 'Let It Be'.

Chapter 3 – 'Ferry Cross the Mersey' by Gerry and the Pacemakers, released as a single in December 1964.

Chapter 4 – 'New Direction' by Echo & the Bunnymen, a track from their 1987 album 'Echo & the Bunnymen'.

Chapter 5 – 'Turn It On' by Ladytron, a track from their 2002 album 'Light & Magic'.

Chapter 6 – 'Dreams Are All We Have' by The Inspiral Carpets, a track from their 1991 album 'The Beast Inside'.

Chapter 7 – 'Day of the Lords' by Joy Division, a track from their 1979 album 'Unknown Pleasures'.

Chapter 8 – 'Up in the Sky' by Oasis, a track from their 1994 album 'Definitely Maybe'.

Chapter 9 – 'Red Frame/White Light' by OMD, a track from their 1980 album 'Orchestral Manoeuvres in the Dark'.

Chapter 10 – 'There Goes the Fear' by Doves, a track from their 2002 album 'The Last Broadcast'.

Chapter 11 – 'Where Flowers Fade' by The Lightning Seeds, a track from their 1992 album 'Sense'.

Chapter 12 – 'Colours Fly Away' by The Teardrop Explodes, a track from their 1981 album 'Wilder'.

Chapter 13 – 'One Day Like This' by Elbow, a track from their 2008 album 'The Seldom Seen Kid'.

Chapter 14 – 'Magic in the Air' by Badly Drawn Boy, from his 2000 album 'The Hour of Bewilderbeast'.

Chapter 15 – 'This Charming Man' by The Smiths, released as a single in October 1983.

Chapter 16 – 'Whole Again' by Atomic Kitten, a track from their 2000 album 'Right Now'.

Chapter 17 – 'I Am the Resurrection' by The Stone Roses, a track from their 1989 Album 'The Stone Roses'.

Acknowledgements and Thanks

Putting this work together has not been a simple task, and there have been times when support and encouragement have been called up. For that I thank Rob Davidson, Nick Evans, John Missenden, Dave Stretton, Brian Thompson, Clive Morris, Leon Pegg, Andrew Humphries, John Winterbottom, John Homer, Mark Bowman and the rest of my colleagues at the Electric Railway Museum. A special thanks to Ali Omar for his request for daily updates on progress, which have kept me on my toes. Also I must thank my children Sarah and Ben – not forgetting Mark, too!

In getting the material ready I have to thank Basil Hancock for once again supplying many, many quality pictures for use, and the same applies to Phil Hughes for not only supplying pictures, but pointing me in the direction of other sources of quality images. I would also like to extend my personal thanks to John Christopher, who first indulged me the idea for writing this book, and finally a huge thank you to everyone working at Amberley Publishing for their support in getting this work into print.

Bibliography

Andrews, H. H., *Electricity in Transport* (The English Electric Company Limited, 1951).

Box, Charles E., *The Liverpool Overhead Railway* (Ian Allan, 1984).

Cooper, B. K., *Electric Trains in Britain* (Ian Allan, 1979).

Dixon, Frank, *The Manchester South Junction & Altrincham Railway* (The Oakwood Press, 1994).

Drewett, Alan, *Electrification Pioneers* on http://glostransporthistory.visit-gloucestershire.co.uk/index.html.

Gahan, John W., *Seaport to Seaside* (Countryvise Limited, 1985).

Gahan, John W., *Steel Wheels to Deeside* (Countryvise Limited, 1983).

Gahan, John W., *The Line Beneath the Liners* (Countryvise Limited, 1983).

Glover, John, *English Electric Traction Album* (Ian Allan, 1981).

Jarvis, Adrian, *Portrait of the Liverpool Overhead Railway* (Ian Allan, 1996).

The London & North Eastern Railway Encyclopedia on www.lner.info.

Mellor, Roger, *Liverpool to Southport Electrification* on www.lyrs.org.uk.

Osborne, Roger, *Iron, Steam & Money – The Making of the Industrial Revolution* (The Bodley Head, 2013).

The Railways Archive, http://www.railwaysarchive.co.uk/, Government and BTC reports.

Rogers, H. B., *The Suburban Growth of Victorian Manchester* on www.mangeogsoc.org.uk.

Vickers, R. L., *DC Electric Trains and Locomotives in the British Isles* (David & Charles, 1986).